C000226501

The Long Hallway

LIVING OUT

Gay and Lesbian Autobiographies

DAVID BERGMAN, JOAN LARKIN, and
RAPHAEL KADUSHIN, *Founding Editors*

The Long Hallway

Richard Scott Larson

THE UNIVERSITY OF WISCONSIN PRESS

Publication of this book has been made possible, in part, through support from the Anonymous Fund of the College of Letters and Science at the University of Wisconsin–Madison.

The University of Wisconsin Press
728 State Street, Suite 443
Madison, Wisconsin 53706
uwpress.wisc.edu

Gray's Inn House, 127 Clerkenwell Road
London EC1R 5DB, United Kingdom
eurospanbookstore.com

Copyright © 2024 by Richard Scott Larson
The Board of Regents of the University of Wisconsin System
All rights reserved. Except in the case of brief quotations embedded in critical articles and reviews, no part of this publication may be reproduced, stored in a retrieval system, transmitted in any format or by any means—digital, electronic, mechanical, photocopying, recording, or otherwise—or conveyed via the Internet or a website without written permission of the University of Wisconsin Press. Rights inquiries should be directed to rights@uwpress.wisc.edu.

Printed in the United States of America
This book may be available in a digital edition.

Library of Congress Cataloging-in-Publication Data

Names: Larson, Richard Scott, author.
Title: The long hallway / Richard Scott Larson.
Other titles: Living out.
Description: Madison, Wisconsin : The University of Wisconsin Press, 2024. | Series: Living out: gay and lesbian autobiographies
Identifiers: LCCN 2023041529 | ISBN 9780299347246 (paperback)
Subjects: LCSH: Larson, Richard Scott. | Halloween (Motion picture : 1978) | Sexual minority men—Biography. | LCGFT: Autobiographies.
Classification: LCC HQ75.8.L377 A3 2024 | DDC 306.760811—dc23/eng/20231030
LC record available at https://lccn.loc.gov/2023041529

For Michael

And pleasure came into his sleep; within
his sleep he sees and possesses the shape, the flesh he wanted . . .

—C. P. CAVAFY, "In the Boring Village" (trans. Daniel Mendelsohn)

He was watching me.

—LAURIE STRODE in *Halloween*

The Long Hallway

1

THE LAST TIME I EVER SAW MY FATHER ALIVE, he wanted to talk to me about girls. I was twelve years old and my father thirty-six, younger even than I am now. We were sitting across from each other in the sun at a picnic table in a public park near the house where I had once lived with him. My mother waited nearby in the car, watching us through the windshield. Cigarette smoke drifted out into the air through the open window, and sometimes her hand would emerge to flick ashes to the ground, the bright red polish on her fingernails catching the sunlight. My little brother was playing alone on a merry-go-round near the line of trees obscuring the recreation area from the outskirts of a suburban housing development, just far enough away that our voices didn't carry over to him when my father broached the subject he had wanted to discuss.

I hadn't seen him in a while. He had lost the old house to foreclosure after the divorce, and my mother told me he'd been staying with friends, living out of a suitcase and moving from couch to couch, trying to figure things out. But he had called earlier that week and asked to see his boys. My mother said he'd even been sober at the time. He had at least seemed sober to me that day in the park, and by then I knew how to tell, because his hands trembled with the effort of trying to keep the hunger inside of him hidden from me. He might have already suspected what I was hiding from him too. Maybe that was why he had called.

My father raised his arm to wave at me as I approached. He was already sitting at the picnic table, wearing an old T-shirt that I recognized with the logo of a local car repair company stitched into the breast pocket, navy sweatpants with a hole at the knee and dark stains deepening the color of the fabric. "Michael Myers," he said with a smile as I slid onto the bench across from him, invoking his nickname for me when I would still visit him at the old house after the rest of us had moved away. The masked murderer from John Carpenter's *Halloween*. My father raised his arm and clenched a fist that we both imagined held a gleaming knife, the blade wet with blood.

Before that Saturday springtime afternoon, I had visited that park only for the annual light show during the holidays with my grandparents. My grandfather would be behind the wheel, inching the car slowly along the brightly decorated drive in a long line of other vehicles, while my brother and I pressed our faces to the windows and took in the displays of holiday lights bringing various figures to life: a group of snowmen standing around a gingerbread house, reindeer in flight dashing up into the trees. But now it was like any other public park: playgrounds and ball fields, new leaves on the trees a dazzling green in the sunlight, so bright I had to shield my eyes just to look at them from where I was sitting. The distant sound of laughing children filled the air. A young couple rowed a paddleboat around a small pond down a hill past the parking lot, and I could smell the smoke from a barbecue, the charcoal cutting through the scent of freshly cut grass as meat sizzled above an open flame.

A mosquito landed near my elbow, and I crushed it with a slap of my palm, leaving a trail of blood on my arm when I wiped it from my skin.

"You said you'd take me to see *Scream*," I said to my father. I'd been waiting for months after obsessing over the trailers on TV—the teenage girl answering the phone in the empty house, all those dark windows looking out to the backyard where someone is spying on her from the shadows, taunting her to the brink of hysteria by letting her know in his cruelly playful way that he's been watching her from outside. That he could see everything. I liked the way his voice sounded over the phone, the way he had distorted it to hide who he really was.

"I think it's still playing at the dollar show," I added hopefully. Everyone at school was talking about it.

"We'll have to ask your mom," said my father. Then he leaned back and looked at me as if he was sizing me up, seeing me for the very first time. "She says you're liking your new school?"

My mother and brother and I had moved into a new house when I started middle school—the second house we had lived in without my father—and now I was in a class with a different group of kids. We'd never lived that far down the highway, where new suburbs filled with cookie-cutter neighborhoods sprawled west past the Missouri River, separating our county from St. Louis. Woods tapered off into desolate flatlands, and then endless fields of wheat and corn stretched into the distance toward the university town in the middle of the state where my mother's aunt lived in a small house in the woods, feral cats prowling the overgrown grass. A farmhouse stood here and there along the interstate, horses and cows resting in sunlit fields just past the edge of the road where a wooden fence kept them from wandering into harm's way. A landscape that did not include my father.

"It's fine," I said. "We're reading *The Hobbit* in English class."

My father smiled at me as he squinted and shielded his eyes with the hand he'd pretended held the knife belonging to Michael Myers. I've always pictured his smile when I've thought of him in the years since then, how the corners of his eyes crinkled up and he pulled his face back over his neck like an actor in a movie pantomiming having been caught unawares. His round cheeks lifted up toward his eyes and a barked laugh often followed, after which he would cough and cover his mouth with the back of his hand before lighting up another cigarette.

"I hope nobody is giving you any trouble," he said finally, the implied question lingering between us. Maybe he'd already pictured me being beaten up by the bigger boys, chased home from the bus stop and scrambling toward the front door of the house. I was all skin and bones, an expression my mother and my father had both used to describe me at the time. I always imagined in those years that I looked easily breakable, like something cheap and poorly made.

I leaned forward over the picnic table with my elbows digging into the wooden planks, pulling my shoulders over my body like I was squeezing myself into the narrow confines of a shell. Then my father was telling me I was going to be a man soon. He sat up straighter, pushed out his chest. He wanted to know how I was doing in that regard and whether I had any questions about what was coming. He referred to the birthday I would celebrate at the end of the summer when I would turn thirteen, a birthday I dreaded for what I thought it meant I would have to do— what the teenagers in movies were always doing. Everything I knew or at least expected of adolescence was that it would involve pursuing girls and trying to lure them into dark corners. The heavy petting I'd seen in those teenage romances always took place in closets.

"I don't know," I said, blushing. I looked away from my father's face. I didn't want to talk about any of this. I was worried that once I started, everything would come spilling out.

I caught myself gazing across the park at a group of older boys playing basketball on a paved court down at the bottom of a small, grassy hill near the pond, their sweaty and shirtless bodies colliding with one another as they scrambled for the ball. Then all I could see in my mind's eye were my hands roaming free over their muscled torsos, slick and wet with the sweat sleeked across their hot skin, already hard when my fingers slipped beneath the elastic waistbands of their shorts and took what I wanted most. When I turned quickly back to my father, I thought he would be able to see it in my face, like film projected onto a blank screen, everything I kept hidden in my mind playing out in plain sight. But he was only continuing to explain that my body would be changing soon and that I needed to have a plan for what was coming, what I'd be turning into.

"You need to be as strong as the other kids," he said. "A time will come when you'll need to defend yourself, if only just to show them that you can."

He asked me to flex my arm for him right there at the picnic table. I'd seen other boys do this at school, slapping their exposed biceps to show off the muscles they'd been cultivating in the basement weight room after the final bell rang each afternoon, while I'd instead be running for the bus, desperate to be alone in my bedroom away from the prying eyes of everyone around me. I bent my right arm at the elbow and squeezed as hard as I could, but my father only smiled weakly and told me I needed to do more push-ups in the morning before school, maybe start lifting dumbbells like the ones he'd kept in the basement in the old house but that I'd never actually seen him pick up. He didn't seem to like my chances when he pictured me standing up to the other boys my age. He didn't see me holding my own.

"What about the girls at your new school?" my father asked. He tried to sound nonchalant, but I sensed that the question made him nervous. This was what he had brought me there to ask. This was what had been worrying him. "Anyone catching your eye?" he continued. He slapped my shoulder playfully. "Any future victims?"

My father had wanted me to be able to charm the girls I passed in the hallways between classes, the same girls I hated for how easily they captivated the boys I secretly watched out of the corners of my eyes. He told me I should join a sports team because the girls were attracted to the uniforms. "Maybe track and field," he said. "I know you're a fast runner." He said I could train all summer and then try out for the team when school started again in the fall. I would get a jacket with the school mascot emblazoned across the back, the outline of a Native American headdress framing the stern face of a powerful chief, my last name spelled out in capital letters that people would be able to read from a mile away.

"You want the girls to come to you first," my father said as he leaned back and crossed his arms. "That way, you're the one in charge."

I could tell he was just worried about me. He only wanted me to be like the other boys because it would be easier for me that way. He wasn't the kind of father to call me names when I couldn't catch a football or laugh at me when I stumbled between bases during a Little League game. He would never have made me feel bad about something I couldn't control. He was only trying to protect me. But he wouldn't have known how to keep me safe from what was coming. I could tell as I met his eyes across the picnic table that he just wanted to be sure I would grow into the right kind of man, but this made me afraid that he would see the kind of man I was actually turning into, the monster inside of me pressing hard against my skin and trying to wriggle its way out.

A girl named Sarah had recently been leaving me handwritten notes expressing her desire to be my girlfriend, and then one day she bravely invited me to a school dance. She was standing next to my locker when I arrived one morning after walking across the parking lot from the bus, her fingers anxiously twining her straight brown hair, and she made awkward small talk while I gathered my textbooks for class. My hands began to tremble when I sensed what she might ask me, and she finally blurted out the question of whether I had already made plans for the dance.

"My mom is buying me a new dress," she said quickly. Then she immediately blushed a deep shade of pink and stared at the floor while the words hung in the air between us, and I felt ashamed then for the first time, not of what I already knew about myself but of what I knew I couldn't offer her.

"I haven't made any plans," I said finally, my voice cracking. And I accepted her invitation because I was afraid of what would happen if I turned her down, failing to play the part I'd been assigned. Everyone at school would wonder why I would rather spend my time alone than dance to loud pop music in a dimly lit gymnasium with a girl like Sarah, the first clue of many that would all add up to a final verdict about what I was.

But when the night came, I pretended to have come down with some kind of flu. I even made my mother call Sarah's house to let her know that I wasn't going to be joining her, because I didn't think I could form the words reliably with my own mouth. I would betray the truth through what I didn't say. I avoided Sarah afterward at school in the most cringingly obvious of ways, and she never asked me out again after spending the night of the dance alone at home, too embarrassed about my rejection to show her face there. I never received another note in my locker. She and I eventually became just two classmates who would pass each other in the hallway with maybe a smile or a small wave, the confusion and hurt in the wake of what had happened never exhumed or made right.

I couldn't tell my father the truth about Sarah that day in the park. "There's one girl," I said haltingly instead, keeping my eyes fixed on the dry leaves stuck between the wooden planks of the picnic table as my mind raced to invent a story.

Later I would tell this same story to kids at school when asked about whether I had a secret crush, someone who occupied the space in my mind reserved for what I wanted most. I would tell the story to kids at summer camp who wanted to know why I never talked to the groups of girls huddled together in revealing bathing suits at the edge of the pool during our allotted swimming time, their pale legs making slow circles in the water as they whispered secrets into each other's ears.

I told my father about an imaginary girl at school whom I had befriended in math class by pretending I couldn't memorize the equations, joking with her before the bell rang each day and then passing notes to her when the teacher wasn't looking. I said I'd even invited her on a date. I told my father I'd asked her out in front of everyone sitting around her at a table in the school cafeteria, suggesting we check out the new ice-skating rink in town. The older sister of a friend of mine worked concessions. We would get free soda all night long. And the imaginary girl told me she would really love to, but she had a boyfriend who went to another school.

"He's already in high school," she said to me in the story I had made up, as if that meant everything.

When I finished telling my lie, I looked up at my father and wondered what I would see in his face—whether the lie would have changed everything between us, revealing me as a fraud and as something so much less than a son. But he was only smiling consolingly when our eyes finally met, and he even reached out and tapped my shoulder across the picnic table in a gesture I recognized as a way for a man to offer support to another man when he's down and out, to make everything okay again. I could tell that my father was proud of me for putting myself out there, making clear what I wanted from this girl who didn't actually exist.

"Everything will work out eventually," he said, visibly relieved. Or at least that's the way he seems now when I remember our last day together. "You'll be in high school before you know it. You know I met your mom in high school."

I glanced over to where I could still see my mother waiting for us in the car. She hadn't even spoken to my father when we pulled into the parking lot. She just looked for a spot in the shade after she saw him waiting for us, and she told us to be careful if we played on the playground. The monkey bars might be slippery from the previous night's rain, a storm I'd watched rage outside my bedroom window while I stayed up until the edges of dawn cracked open the night sky and the other houses in the neighborhood all appeared again out of the darkness, front lawns glistening from the rainfall. Then she pressed the button to unlock the doors in the back seat, and out we went. My mother told me to keep an eye on my brother, as she lit a cigarette and turned the dial on the radio to find a station playing old rock music, and I quietly stepped out of the car onto the hot pavement and walked toward my father.

"There's a girl out there for you," he said finally. "You'll find her someday."

He called my brother over from the merry-go-round, and the three of us ate potato chips from a bag my father had brought with him. We talked about video games and scary movies. Eventually my mother

9

honked the car horn, indicating that it was time for us to go. She was in a bowling league on Saturday nights with her new boyfriend, and she had to get ready before we left for the long drive down the highway from our house. He lived several towns over. The sun was already about to go down.

We stood up from the bench and went around to the other side of the picnic table to hug our father goodbye. My brother was already scrambling toward my mother's car when my father hooked one arm around me and I was enveloped for the last time in the smell of the old cigarette smoke clinging to his clothing and skin. There was a sour trace of the beer he must have spilled on the shirt the last time he'd worn it, and I was immediately transported in my mind back to his house on those long afternoons I'd spent in front of his TV watching the rented copy of *Halloween*, my father sitting just around the corner at the kitchen table every time the familiar soundtrack began to play, his hand always curled around a can of beer.

He still smelled like the old house. But the old house was gone.

I was opening the door to the back seat of my mother's car when I heard my father call again from where he was still sitting at the picnic table. "Michael Myers," he said, and I instinctively turned back to face him. He raised his hand, and I did the same. A goodbye gesture. I never saw him again.

My father never knew the true story playing out behind the anxious eyes of the boy who had lied to him that day in the park. To him I would always be his quiet and secretive son who couldn't stop watching the man in the mask holding the bloody knife. But the boy who walked away from him that day in the park was grateful to be finished with the conversation he had started, desperate to shed and leave behind forever the words we'd shared.

My father had said there was a girl out there for me, but I couldn't have known how soon after that day she would come into my life. And I didn't know yet that she would be a dead girl.

~

The day I heard the news began like any other. It was a Monday morning just after dawn, my mother flashing the overhead light in my bedroom on and off with impatient flicks of the switch by the doorway as I finally opened my eyes after tossing and turning most of the night.

"You slept through your alarm again," she said. I squinted and saw her tired face in the doorway between my closet door and a poster on the wall for one of the *Texas Chainsaw Massacre* sequels. She hadn't put on her makeup yet, and I saw that her hair was still wet from the shower, clinging to her skull like a swim cap, only her bangs in curlers. "The sound that thing makes could raise the dead. I heard it all the way down the hall."

I was having the dream every night by then—the dream about the man waiting for me at the end of the long hallway. The walls were porous, alive and breathing, and as I walked toward the man whom I could only ever barely discern far ahead of me in the shadows, I was unable to stop myself from moving forward, regardless of how much I feared the consequences of every step. Along the wall I passed people with blurred faces and frightened eyes who would kill themselves in some elaborately gruesome way just as my gaze met theirs. Some held sharp knives that they plunged deep into their chests without hesitation as I drew near. Some were able to strangle themselves to death with a rope or a belt in the few seconds it took for me to move on to the next person in line. And some were already close to death, choking or wheezing or doubled over in agony before collapsing to the ground. But even though I knew that each person would die immediately after I passed by, I couldn't bring myself to stop walking forward. A scream would build and build in my throat as I realized I would soon have to confront the man at the end of the hallway, but so far I had never reached him before I managed to shake myself awake.

This time my mother had saved me. I winced at the flash of the bulb above my bed and pulled the blanket over my face, my eyes still heavy with sleep.

"You're going to miss the bus," my mother was saying, and I finally pulled myself up into a sitting position. She was standing in the door-way dressed for work in one of the skirt-and-blouse combinations that her boss liked. My brother rushed past her on his way downstairs for breakfast. I could smell the shampoo from his shower, caught a glimpse of the bright neon yellow of his backpack as he disappeared down the stairs.

"I don't have time to drive you again," my mother continued. She pushed the door all the way open and walked back down to her own bedroom only when my bare feet were finally planted firmly on the carpet next to my bed, the man from the dream fading from my mind as I stood up and rummaged in my closet for something to wear. I glanced out my bedroom window and saw cars already pulling out of driveways, the headlights from the highway near the entrance to the neighborhood flashing bright through the trees.

The bus ride to school was always loud and chaotic, high school kids throwing sharpened pencils toward the front when the driver wasn't looking and younger kids screaming and bursting into tears when the backs of their necks got nicked. I would shrink against the window and imagine myself somewhere far away, trying to make myself invisible as I counted down the minutes. That morning my mother managed to shove us out the front door just before the bus pulled up, waving for the driver to wait for us to scramble down the driveway. I turned back before climbing up the steps, but she was already in the car with the garage door open, the brake lights coming on as she turned the key in the ignition.

I braced myself for the assault of voices slicing through the air, bodies and backpacks pressed against each other on the cushioned benches. But as I slid into the first available seat, I realized no one was talking at all. The girl next to me had her face pressed to the window with her eyes staring blankly ahead. One of the older boys across the aisle was playing a handheld video game, and the occasional burst of electronic sound was all I could hear. The bus driver—a retired math teacher with long gray hair in a ponytail, who sometimes clipped the side mirrors of parked cars—met my eyes in the mirror as I sat down. She shook her head slowly from side to side as if to say that it was terrible, so terrible—whatever it was that had happened. This thing I didn't know. And when I walked into the middle-school building, I saw that everyone was huddled in groups by their lockers, their voices hushed and solemn.

A girl from my class was crying silently, long streaks of eyeliner marking her otherwise pale face. A boy who played on the eighth-grade basketball team tried to comfort her by touching her shoulder, but she let out a loud sob and disappeared into the girls' restroom, the door slamming shut behind her.

I grabbed my textbooks from my locker and walked to my first class without waiting for the bell. The desks and chairs around mine gradually became occupied until the English teacher finally stood up from her desk, where she'd been fidgeting with a stack of pencils while the students filed in, and quietly pulled the classroom door shut as we waited silently for the morning announcements to begin. I didn't notice the empty desk in front of me until the principal's voice came over the intercom in the corner, a sharp buzz as the speaker crackled to life. He cleared his throat and then said gravely, "I'm sure you've already heard what happened."

But I still didn't know. No one had told me anything. I'd spent the previous day alone in my room, locked away with my paperback books and whatever horror film I'd rented for myself at the video store, probably something with a serial killer. And my brother and I had spent the rest of Saturday night after the visit with our father shooting darts in the basement of our mother's boyfriend's house and then dozing on the couch while a professional wrestling match played on the screen. "Look at all that blood on his face," my mother had said when they got home and woke us up, greasy fast food waiting in a paper bag as the broadcast came to its inevitable conclusion. By then the blood was the only thing I could see.

The others in my class were all staring straight ahead when the principal finally delivered the news. "I know this is difficult to hear," he said. "We all loved her very much."

He told us that the girl—a girl named T, who normally sat in front of me in class—had been murdered late Saturday night and that her body had been found early the next morning. He held a long pause as if waiting for us to absorb the news, the faint crackle of the speaker in the corner of the room the only evidence that he was still there with us. Then he said that counselors were available in the guidance office if we needed to talk to someone in the wake of what had happened. We would be notified of funeral arrangements. We could call our parents if we wanted to be excused from class for the day.

"I'm so sorry," he said finally. "She was a very special girl."

I was holding my copy of *The Hobbit*. A gray-robed wizard on the cover was approaching a hole in the ground from which he would unearth the novel's improbable hero, a diminutive fellow famously averse to adventure. And as the news of T's death entered the classroom, I remember absently wondering how far into the book she'd gotten before her final moments. Whether she had seen Bilbo past the great battle and back to the safety of home, or whether she had left him behind still toiling in the dark of Smaug's lair, scared and alone, unsure whether the future held for him even the remotest possibility of escape.

I hadn't known T well, but I'd observed her at school without speaking to her despite our proximity, her head never even turning my way as she passed stacks of handouts back to me in class. I suspected I would have been unworthy of her company, the shy and skinny and quiet boy I was, so I hung back and watched her from afar, imagining what life might be like in her shoes. Her dark and wavy brown hair was the color of her half-moon eyes, and her cheekbones formed a triangle pointing sharply down to her chin. We had lockers in the same hallway, hers a few classroom doors down from mine, and I would look on while she laughed and charmed everyone with a teasing smile that always seemed to be hiding something. Or so I imagined in retrospect—some secret about who she became outside the walls of the school building. And I thought hearing the news of T's death meant that the story must be over. I didn't realize yet that another story had only just begun.

We weren't told details about the circumstances of her death at school, and I hadn't been included in whatever game of telephone had led to almost everyone but me hearing about it before school that day. But the local TV news channels were already covering the story in depth, as I would discover that night at home. After all, nothing like the murder of a child had ever happened where we lived, a sea of newly built suburban neighborhoods clustered around highway exits stretching ever farther west, away from the city that all our parents insisted was lawless and dangerous. Gas grills, swing sets, and plastic swimming pools crowded the backyards of those cheaply built houses. Young oaks grew on the gentle slopes of freshly mowed front lawns. The local news usually covered only the grand openings of highway extensions and newly constructed bridges, weather forecasts, and brief features about the minor successes of our school sports teams. Nothing ever suggested even the remotest possibility of the horror story that T had stumbled into.

I wondered if my father had already heard about it and whether he might have suspected that T was the girl I'd told him about—the imaginary girl with the older boyfriend who turned me down when I'd asked for a date. The possibility made me squirm with shame—I'd conjured her up from nothing only for her to disappear in the blink of an eye.

And when I turned on the TV above the small kitchen cabinet while my mother microwaved our frozen dinners later that night, I saw T's face in fuzzy close-up from the school picture we had all dutifully lined up for one day last fall. Her hair had been curled for the photograph, and she lifted her chin to smile for the camera.

A female newscaster updated viewers about what had happened to T. The investigation had been unfolding ever since her body had been found early the day before, an otherwise quiet Sunday morning in spring, along the footpaths of a wooded college campus on the other side of the county. T had been raped by her killer before he stabbed her to death, a fact that shocked me into a near paralysis as I realized I hadn't yet pictured how any of it had happened, the details now quickly forming grisly images in my mind. And that was also when I found out that her killer hadn't been caught.

I don't know why I had assumed that someone was already in custody for the crime, safely off the streets and behind bars, no longer a threat. Unsolved murders belonged on sensational late-night TV shows or in the cheap tabloids that my mother sometimes flipped through while waiting in the grocery store checkout line. Things like that happened in faraway places operating under a different set of rules than the ones we followed in our small town. I wondered then whether she was only the first dead girl in what would be a series of dead girls, the beginning rather than the end of the story. The darkness outside my bedroom window after I learned about T's murder now held some kind of latent possibility of someone hiding out there so that no one would discover what he really was and come to punish him for it. And I realized with a familiar sense of almost unbearable tension that I couldn't wait to see what would happen next, just as in the horror movies I watched back then with a morbid fascination, carefully tracing the movements of the killer through ever-darkening shadows until the very last scene where the last girl alive faces her bogeyman.

The story of the unsolved murder—so often the story of a dead girl— is told backward, exhumed from the past during an investigation taking place in the present. The clues unearthed by investigators slowly paint a picture of the dead girl that no one could have guessed at before— trouble she'd gotten into that she had kept secret until now, mistakes she might have made that had led to this tragic end. The story moves forward only as it gradually reveals what came before, when the girl was still alive and only beginning to stumble into the circumstances that would lead to her demise.

The story of the dead girl has by necessity already happened before the real story about the investigation can begin. She can only sit by and watch it unfold.

At the time I learned about T's murder, I was still living inside my own kind of story that was always moving forward without me. The secret I was keeping about myself had trapped me in a holding pattern, an endless series of false starts that each led me right back to the same place—alone in my dark bedroom, always late at night, waiting for the day when I could finally take those few halting steps into the future, just as I did each night in the long hallway in my dream. I couldn't imagine what that day would look like, but it loomed in the distance like the edge of an abyss that I would either leap over or be swallowed up by completely.

I imagined I would soon be plucked from the crowd and named for what I was. The images playing out behind my eyes as I began to secretly name my desires would be broadcast in the school auditorium for everyone to hear, the other boys seeing themselves portrayed in my mind's eye in ways that would make them want to destroy me, just as someone had destroyed T. Maybe I didn't necessarily want her murder to be solved and the world to be set right as much as I wanted to slip into her skin and take what she might share with me, empty herself of the memories of what had happened to her so that I could shoulder them myself. I'd endlessly rewind and replay the story of the dead girl in my mind, my stomach roiling with shame even as I relished the imagined feeling of being desired and hunted, relentlessly pursued until I could feel a man's breath hot on the back of my neck as he closed in.

After all, I'd been studying the man in the mask. I knew what happened next.

2

I watched *Halloween* for the first time in my father's living room during one of the weekends when I was visiting him at the old house where we had all lived before the divorce. I was only nine years old—three years before the day in the park when I'd see my father for the last time—and my bare knees were pressed into the brittle brown carpet as I was transported and initiated into the world of Michael Myers. The smoke from my father's cigarettes wafted in from the kitchen around the corner where he sat at a folding card table watching a Cardinals game on the smaller black-and-white TV above the liquor cabinet. I was alone, crouched down in the next room, my face drifting closer and closer to the screen as darkness fell outside, where young parents pushed strollers and walked their dogs before heading inside for the evening.

My father had the volume of the baseball game turned down low enough in the room next door that I could hear only *Halloween*'s cryptic soundtrack, my body tense and charged as the film descended seductively into a kind of darkness that felt to me like the perfect place to hide. And in the days and months that followed, I would watch *Halloween* at my father's house whenever I could, sometimes even rewinding it immediately after the final credits finished rolling just to start it all over again, everything happening backward as I held down the button on the VCR. A Halloween night in reverse, the oversized plastic bags and pillowcases in the arms of the costumed trick-or-treaters being emptied rather than filled. Each of Michael's victims coming back to life one by one and walking in reverse down the tree-lined sidewalks, moving away from rather than toward their fates, oblivious to the nature of the story in which they would soon find themselves.

My father had driven us to the video store in town earlier that afternoon, and we came back home with a rented copy of the film. I'd wandered the aisles of the store alone while my father waited in the car, nursing one of the beers he always brought with him for even the shortest of drives, steering the car with one hand while the other clutched a gently crumpled can. I could see him waiting for me through the store's large front window overlooking the parking lot and our town's quiet commercial Main Street. His arm was extended out the driver's-side window as he flicked ashes onto the parking lot pavement and other customers came and went. My brother was still sitting in the back seat huddled over the handheld video game he'd gotten for his birthday earlier in the summer, his bobbing head like a mirage through the smoke from my father's cigarettes. Sometimes I'd see him glance up and squint toward the store window, perhaps wondering what was taking me so long. But I always took my time, inspecting every film on the metal racks before making my selection.

I finally came upon a copy of *Halloween* that day in a Horror aisle that I'd explored many times before, the glowing eyes of vampires and werewolves lingering on me as I took each step forward on the red carpeted floor. I'd already exhausted several of the popular summer-camp slasher franchises and the old black-and-white monster movies, terrified women cowering in the shadow of a creature lurking just off-screen. And I was immediately entranced and drawn in by the haunting simplicity of *Halloween*'s cover image, a viciously grinning jack-o'-lantern seeming to grip the exaggeratedly angled blade of a knife, the fire inside the face of the pumpkin visible only through the carved-out holes of its eyes. I wanted to know what it saw.

The image on the video case reminded me of the well-worn paperbacks lining my mother's bookshelves in her bedroom, mostly cheap and mass market, the bindings frayed and the pages already yellowed with age. The covers of these novels featured eyes glowing in perfect darkness, headlights appearing in the foggy distance on an otherwise empty street. Or maybe a dark house on a stark hilltop beneath a stormy sky with only the uppermost attic window glowing bright, as if to convey that the person inside was to be kept hidden upstairs and perpetually out of sight. I would sneak these paperbacks from my mother's bedroom into my own like contraband, reading them by flashlight on nights when sleep didn't come easily. Most nights. I was supposed to be reading books about chosen ones embarking upon quests to save imaginary worlds, sports heroes or mysteries soon to be solved by resourceful boy detectives. I was supposed to be reading stories with happy endings. But I already knew that what interested me in the world was also what scared me—the unexplainable, the supernatural, characters suffering random violence at the hands of strangers.

My brother was sprawled across the twin mattress down the hall in his old bedroom playing his video game as the film began, so I was alone in front of the TV as I watched the opening credits of *Halloween* for the first time, the camera slowly zeroing in on the vaguely triangular shape of a jack-o'-lantern's perfectly carved eye. My heart was already thudding in my chest as day turned to night outside the living room window in our sprawling suburban neighborhood, the streetlights winking on all down the block like the streetlights in Haddonfield, Illinois, a town that looked just like mine and where Michael Myers lurked in the shadows.

The first shot of the film reveals an innocuous white two-story suburban house at nighttime. A welcoming front porch is complete with a jack-o'-lantern glowing from atop a small table next to the living room window, neatly trimmed hedges and bushes, a sprinkling of fallen leaves scattered across the sidewalk. And only when the camera begins to approach the front porch did I realize that I was actually looking through the eyes of a particular character in the scene. The six-year-old Michael Myers has just returned from trick-or-treating when he sees his sister and a young man locked in a passionate embrace behind the drapes covering the window on the front door. Michael's gaze follows the two lustful teenagers as they move into the living room, and his sister giggles playfully as she leans back into the couch cushions while her boyfriend presses his body against hers from above.

I clenched my fists as I watched through Michael's eyes as his sister's boyfriend picks up a clown mask and kisses her from the other side of the colorful plastic, pressing it roughly against her cheeks. "Take off that face," she insists, and the boyfriend tosses the mask aside—the mask that I later saw would complete Michael's own costume—before suggesting that the two of them head upstairs. Then the first note of the haunting score is struck just as Michael sees the lights wink out in the window of his sister's bedroom above him. A threshold has been crossed, and something has been awakened inside of him. He isn't the same little boy anymore.

Michael enters the house through a back entrance leading into the dark, shadowy kitchen, where he retrieves a knife from a drawer and proceeds to move slowly through the quiet and shadowed hallways. His sister's boyfriend eventually bounds back down the stairs and out the front door, casually pulling on a striped T-shirt over a perfectly toned chest and torso before he dashes back out into the night. Michael then carefully takes his place, quietly retracing the young man's steps up the darkened staircase toward the bedroom where his sister is now alone. He even picks up and dons the discarded clown mask, perhaps having returned home after realizing he'd forgotten it.

The frame is now limited to what can be glimpsed from behind the individual eyeholes of the mask as Michael steps into the bedroom. Clothes are strewn across the floor in what must have been a hasty undressing, and his sister sits topless in her underwear at a vanity table singing quietly to herself while brushing her hair by lamplight. Michael notices that the bedsheets are messily ruffled, evidence of an exchange he doesn't yet understand but for which he intuitively believes she must be punished. The revelation of sexual desire seems to have triggered a latent evil inside Michael's young body that finds expression in the shiny blade of a kitchen knife, my first glimpse of what will become his weapon of choice. Michael hacks his screaming sister to shreds immediately after I hear her cry out his name, and then he slowly and methodically follows in her boyfriend's footsteps down the staircase and out the front door.

My eyes widened as the blade of his knife caught the light.

~

Around the time that I first became acquainted with Michael Myers, my mother began dating for the first time since the divorce. A few times we met a man she'd been seeing at the pizza place in the strip mall by the grocery store in town. Once, he came over for a dinner of spaghetti and garlic bread, my mother cooking while my brother and I sat at the table finishing homework handouts. I glanced up at the man now and then as he stood across the room by the stove as the nightly news played on the small TV in the corner, nursing a beer from a bottle he'd cracked open using the edge of the kitchen counter. My mother had taken a second job bartending a couple weekend shifts at a dive by the highway to make up for the child support payments that my father never sent, and that was where she had met this new man, a customer whom she eventually invited home.

I remember my father always being between jobs at the time, never sustaining anything for long before he drank himself out of work yet again. The jobs he landed always seemed vague to me because they never became anything permanent, so when my mother came home on Fridays from her day job as an accountant's assistant, she shed her skirt and blouse and pulled on the black leggings and low-cut spandex top that she told me was good for tips. I would watch her from the corner of her bed while she made herself up at the vanity table in the corner of her bedroom, painting on the bright green eye shadow that matched the tinted contacts that she always wore, dusting powder over her cheekbones to make them seem even higher and sharper. Tiny light bulbs circled the mirror that she leaned toward closely while inspecting every last touch. Then she would drop my brother and me off at our grandparents' house for the night before driving the short distance to the bar alone.

I must have seemed strange to my mother, an oddity—or at least how that's how I imagine it when I look back and picture the scene. The nervous mother of the sensitive boy, afraid of what she doesn't know about the world of the imagination where he lives without her. The creases on her face deepen as she frowns and squints and inspects the unreadable boy sitting cross-legged on the bed, his body thin and vulnerable, a disposition that already seems almost haunted as he watches her with an intensity she doesn't yet understand.

I used to make a game of hiding from my mother when she came to pick me up from after-school day care. She had to work long hours at the accounting firm, so my brother and I were always among the last kids there. I would spend my time reading alone in a corner of the basement or hiding in the sprawling jungle gym, in the tree house at the top where you could see inside only through a small window carved into the wooden planks. I would pretend not to hear when the employee staying late that day called my name, and while my brother waited patiently with his lunch box and backpack in the lobby, my mother began the search. She always looked in the usual places and had learned over time to find me without much effort, so one day I decided to slip into the broom closet. I sat down and pressed my back against the wall in the dark, pulling my knees to my chest and counting the seconds until the door would be flung open. I waited there for what seemed like far too long, and when I finally came out to the lobby, my mother was sobbing in a corner and being comforted by the secretary while everyone else was overturning the furniture, opening kitchen cupboards, and cursing my ongoing games of evasion.

I knew then that this was a form of torture for my mother, this pretending to be lost, even though I always yearned for the moment when she would find me.

While I watched my mother get ready for the bar, she would tell me about the other women she worked with. She told me about the one with the boyfriend who would stop in for free beers and then get angry when another man took her attention away by ordering a drink. She told me about the one who sometimes cried inconsolably in the back room when a customer looked too much like her father. She told me how the regulars all had their favorites and would always leave a little bit extra in exchange for a returned smile or the slightest touch of a hand when delivering a fresh pour. She told me the women would laugh together while closing the bar at the end of the night, swaying a bit after downing the shots they weren't allowed to refuse when purchased by a paying customer, sometimes calling a cab for one who had drunk too much during her shift. Or sometimes simply sending her off into the arms of the man who had gotten her that way, unable to intervene as she disappeared out the door.

Most of the customers were men, my mother said, unless one of them had a girlfriend who had grudgingly tagged along. I hadn't ever been inside a bar, but I'd seen how they looked in movies—the dark corners where dusty jukeboxes waited for coins, the bright neon lights above the rows of bottles behind the counter. Young women who meant business mixed cocktails in shiny metal shakers and carried trays of beers and shots of brown liquor toward tables full of loud, waiting men, whose faces would be upturned and glowing upon their arrival. In my mind's eye I saw sparkling mirrors adorning each wall, dazzling balls of light dangling from the ceiling like Christmas ornaments. Loud music and a crowded dance floor, everyone looking their best.

I was proud when I imagined my mother in a place like that, the brightness of her smile lighting up all the dark corners. She told me she'd been beautiful in high school, more beautiful than all the other girls, before she married my father just two months after the end of her senior year. She said it like something she no longer was. But she was still beautiful to me, even after what my father had done to her in those last years in his house. She had briefly worked as a catalog model when she was sixteen years old, and I'd seen the photographs of her in advertisements. My grandmother once carefully unfolded the magazine pages from an album she kept almost as a tribute to my mother's youth—my mother before my father. And I knew without setting foot in the bar that she would have been favored by all the men who drank there. I wanted to ask her how it felt to have all those eyes on her, men turning their heads and begging for more when she offered a grazing of her fingertips on their muscled shoulders and asked whether they wanted another round. I was desperate to know what it felt like to have them all in the palm of her hand.

~

One night I was asleep on the top bunk in the bedroom I shared with my brother, who was still snoring softly in the bunk below, when I woke to voices downstairs in the kitchen. My mother had been alone when I went to bed, but now her sudden burst of high-pitched laughter was answered by a man's low voice asking whether she had anything harder than beer.

I remembered the time a man had followed my mother home from her shift at the bar. She told me later that she'd seen his car behind hers when she pulled out of the parking lot and tried her best to lose him, driving down random side streets until she no longer saw his headlights in the rearview mirror. She picked us up from our grandparents' house that night even later than usual. We slept in the back seat all the way home, and we were already upstairs in bed when I heard my mother cry out in alarm. I rushed out of my room, hurried down the stairs, almost tripping over the legs of my oversized pajamas, and stopped short when I saw a man outside the sliding door to our deck. He had parked outside the garage below the deck and climbed onto the top of his car to pull himself up, and now he could see into our kitchen, all the way down the hall where I'd frozen at the foot of the stairs. He must have followed my mother to my grandparents' house, waited outside while she ushered us into the car, then continued behind us down the highway all the way home.

My mother laughed when she told the story later to her friends over the phone while I sat on the stool next to the small kitchen TV where we watched morning cartoons over breakfast, a long Virginia Slims cigarette always swirling smoke around her face while she held the receiver to her ear at the window above the sink, her own reflection staring back at her. But that night, with the strange man on the other side of our sliding door, she had screamed at him to go away, waving me back upstairs and yelling for me to lock the door to my bedroom until she said it was safe to come out. Only when she called the police did the man finally leave, lowering himself back down from the deck after shouting that my mother was a bitch and a tease and then finally driving away. When she came upstairs for bed, I pretended to have already fallen asleep. I pretended I hadn't heard her crying downstairs, maybe looking out the kitchen window to see what trouble might be coming our way next time.

But now on the night when I was woken by my mother's laughter with the man she had willingly invited inside, I listened to her tease him as he spoke to her in a muffled voice that I could tell was already thick with booze, remembering how my father always sounded when he came home late from the bar. This man didn't sound angry or upset, though, and my mother was seemingly unafraid—she wanted him there. And once again I pretended to be asleep when my mother came upstairs with the man whom I finally recognized as the one she'd recently been dating. She pulled him by the hand into her own bedroom across the hallway from mine and closed the door as quietly as she could behind them. I heard the click of the lock. And I was still awake when the door opened later, the man stepping out unsteadily into the half-light of the hallway wearing only his underwear, tight red briefs with a white waistband.

This man was taller and leaner than my father, having a slender build with gently curved muscles lining his arms and legs. My father's torso had already begun to swell like a beach ball despite his otherwise small frame, his belly expanding ever outward as he drank beer after beer at his kitchen table. The man in the hallway paused for his eyes to adjust to the light without knowing I was watching. I'd stolen candy from the gas station on the road between my father's neighborhood and ours, and I remembered that the sweetness melting in my mouth and coloring my tongue bright red was even better when it was something I hadn't paid for. The pleasure I felt at watching this man unseen in the dark was like running all the way home with my pockets full before anyone could punish me for what I'd done.

When he finally began walking toward the bathroom, I couldn't take my eyes off the gentle curve of his lower back arching down past the waistband of his underwear, staring wide-eyed until he had disappeared from sight. I felt my body stir in a way that was at that time still unfamiliar, yet already something I knew I wouldn't be able to control. He didn't bother to close the bathroom door behind him, and I couldn't see him at all around the corner from my bed, but I pictured his stance. His roughly calloused hand would be holding himself firmly while he looked at his body in the mirror, admiring the muscles of his naked chest, rubbing a palm along his jawline, or absently running his fingers down his stomach. He would wink at his reflection before turning off the light.

I held my body rigid and still on my thin mattress and watched as he slipped back into my mother's bedroom, releasing the breath I'd been holding only when he shut the door roughly behind him. I thought I would die if he caught me looking. And I couldn't sleep after that. Just knowing he was there across the hall made it impossible. The darkness around me deepened as my thoughts raced, my face hot against my pillow as I played the scene over and over again in my mind. The sight of the man's body had cracked me open.

That was the first time I knew.

⁓

Before my mother and the man downstairs had woken me up that night, I'd probably been in the dream about the man waiting for me at the end of the long hallway. The dream had only just begun to haunt my nights around that time, but I already knew the rules of the world in which I found myself every time I closed my eyes. The people along the walls dying all those painful deaths, their eyes catching mine before they collapsed to the ground. The fate awaiting me at the hands of the man whom I couldn't help walking toward through the endless darkness, despite the horrors I left in my wake.

The next morning, I was eating a bowl of cereal alone at the kitchen table when the man from the night before came downstairs. I had heard his heavy footsteps moving back and forth between my mother's bedroom and the bathroom, and then my whole body tensed with anticipation when I heard him descending the staircase.

I watched as he turned the corner toward the kitchen, my hand frozen in a fist around my plastic spoon. I could see him from where I always sat at the table for breakfast, my back to the sliding door to the deck and my eyes cast to the right toward the small TV in the corner, a cartoon rerun playing at low volume. My mother must have still been getting ready for work upstairs. Sometimes I would help her choose her work outfit if I finished breakfast in time, scampering up to brush my teeth and watch her prepare to leave for the office. I imagined her already in one of her neatly pressed plaid skirts, buttoning a blouse and choosing a pair of earrings.

The man from the night before was still shirtless, but he had pulled on a pair of dirty jeans that now hung loose around his hips, the waistband of his underwear still clearly visible below the vertical band of muscle framing the sides of his abdomen. I remembered that he worked as a landscaper. The jeans slid down with each step he took, and he hooked a finger into his belt loop to keep them up. He nodded at me with a quick smile as he reached into the refrigerator and pulled out a carton of milk, helping himself to a glass from the drying rack by the sink and downing the milk he'd poured in a few strong gulps before wiping his lips with the back of his hand.

"Little man," he said as he leaned his weight against the counter. My hand trembled around my spoon and I stared into my bowl to keep him from noticing where my gaze would otherwise linger. "Looking sharp. Ready for school?"

I nodded without meeting his eyes. What I wanted instead was for him to sit down next to me at the table and let me breathe in the sweaty scent of him as he leaned closer and closer toward me, his hand finally cupping my chin and gently tilting my face up to meet his eyes. My heart would be pounding while he stroked the side of my neck down to my clavicle, the tickle of his fingertips on my exposed skin igniting something deep inside my body and sending my heart into a deafening roar. But I had him to myself for only a few moments before my mother came downstairs, yelling up the staircase for my brother to finish getting ready for school. She emerged from around the corner of the staircase still wearing only her thin nightgown.

"You must have gotten up early," she said to me, but she wasn't looking in my direction at all. Her eyes had jumped past me like a piece of old furniture. The shirtless man holding the empty glass commanded her complete attention. He hooked another finger into his belt loop and raised an eyebrow at her, scanning my mother up and down in the early morning light slanting in through the kitchen window, his lips turning up in a smile.

My mother had made me invisible, scrubbed the room clean of my presence. This man had never given me a second glance at the pizza place or during the single time he'd previously come to our house. But that was before I cared at all about his attention—before I'd seen him so completely, his body there for the taking. Now I wanted him to finally notice me that morning in the kitchen, my cereal growing soggy in the plastic bowl with my name written inside a balloon drawn across the bottom. A child's cereal bowl. I was just a child. There was nothing I had that this man wanted. My mother only had to walk into the room for him to forget all about me. She barely had to do anything at all.

~

At the end of the opening sequence of *Halloween*, the young Michael Myers steps outside his family's house and approaches the street just as his parents emerge from a car parked at the curb, having returned from a night on the town. His father comes around the hood of the car and calls to him questioningly and suspiciously, as if he doesn't recognize what his own son has become. But instead of immediately relieving him of the bloodied knife, his father first removes the mask that Michael had worn as he claimed the first of what would be his many future victims. The imperative isn't to immediately disarm the costumed Michael Myers of a murder weapon. Rather, it's to reveal him. To show his face.

Michael is wearing a cheap clown costume probably purchased for him by his mother. His dirty blond hair is disheveled, his eyes blank as he stares at something just past the camera—or maybe at nothing at all, his perspective without the mask unreadable by anyone but himself.

He seems to be in a state of shock, not yet realizing what he's done. Or perhaps not realizing its irrevocability, what it means for him to have done it. The camera then suddenly pulls back and soars high up into the night sky to establish the context of the quiet suburban neighborhood in which Michael lives, as if to suggest that there might be others out there just like him and that they could be living closer to our own homes than we might have ever imagined.

Michael has only been doing what felt natural to him at the time, following his newly discovered desire to its inevitable conclusion. He doesn't understand yet that he is going to be punished for what he has revealed to the world about himself.

The opening of *Halloween* is a coming-out story.

3

WHEN I FIRST WATCHED MICHAEL MYERS stalking the streets of Haddonfield, my father was already slurring his words and coughing up cigarette smoke in the kitchen on the other side of the wall from where I sat, the smell of beer hanging always in the air. Sometimes I would carefully stack the empty cans tossed into the bin in the garage and imagine them as the walls of a fort, my own secret domain where I'd hide with one of my books for hours, growing gradually accustomed to the sour stench of the dregs at the bottom of each can. I'd once taken a beer from the box when my father wasn't looking and drank it by myself alone in my old bedroom. I wanted to see what it was like to do what he did. I gulped it down and then I lay on my back across my bare mattress and watched the ceiling swirl in and out of focus, my head spinning as if I was on a carnival ride at the county fair. Eventually I felt too dizzy and sick to even keep my eyes open, and I just waited for everything to run its course.

I was able to watch *Halloween* on what sometimes felt like an endless loop after that first viewing because my father never returned it to the video store. The VHS tape and its blue plastic box remained at the house long after the due date had been forgotten, the small white label on the otherwise featureless container revealing only the name of the film, the year of its release, and its genre: *horror*, a word that would come to imply a kind of comfort for me throughout my childhood and adolescence, an increasingly necessary escape from the real.

Maybe my father had recognized how the film had activated something in my imagination and kept it in the house to encourage me to visit him more often, already sensing my increasing reluctance to do so in the years following the divorce. I might have even asked him myself if we could keep the tape and never return it to the video store. Maybe I couldn't bear to part with it, not understanding then that we could simply buy our own copy. It's more likely, however, that my father completely forgot how the old, beat-up tape had found its way into his house. After all, I had used my mother's account when I checked out with the cashier, so my father really had no incentive to make the trip to return it. And I assume she quietly paid the inevitable fine on my father's behalf, having learned by then to pick her battles when it came to what he owed her.

I wondered sometimes what I looked like to my father on those long afternoons with my eyes glued to the screen, so enthralled by all those teenagers being hunted down by an inscrutable masked villain—hands under my knees, my upper body slumped forward in the direction of the television, my back gently curved inward. I wondered whether he saw me as I saw myself—a future victim, too gentle to survive adolescence unscathed. Maybe that's how he saw me that last day in the park when he tried to talk to me about girls, like a child in a fairy tale wandering off alone into the woods. For me, *Halloween* had become a kind of fairy tale from the very beginning, a portal through which I could walk right into Haddonfield. The plot was simple enough to allow me to imagine myself into it and all the ways in which I might have intervened.

After the opening flashback sequence, the film follows two adolescent babysitters and one of their friends from high school as they are stalked and hunted on Halloween night by a madman on the loose in the small town where he'd once committed a heinous crime. We find out very little about Laurie, Annie, and Lynda aside from minor details that explain how Michael is able to pursue them. We're not supposed to *care* about these girls, necessarily, but rather to identify with them, to become them—if only for the duration of the scenes in which they confront the bogeyman. Yet that day in the living room of my father's house I became not Laurie running for her life but Michael watching her from the shadows. I couldn't stop thinking about the shirtless man I'd seen in the hallway stepping out of my mother's bedroom in the dead of night, the contours of his body already seared forever into memory, even though I never saw him again. My mother stopped seeing him after an argument about his drinking that reminded her too much of being with my father. But every thought of him was a jolt at my core reminding me what I had invited inside.

~

A little boy of maybe four or five years old is alone in a pumpkin patch on a sunny autumn day wearing blue jeans and a bright blue coat zipped up to his neck, glancing shyly into the camera when someone calls his name. His straight blond hair sometimes falls into his eyes, and he distractedly swipes it away with a gloved hand. The little boy is standing between two long rows of pumpkins, inspecting each one as he walks slowly away from the man holding the camera, the ground beneath his feet strewn with newly fallen autumn leaves. Later he will stand next to a scarecrow and pick at the straw of its chest, the red flannel shirt affixed to its makeshift body billowing lightly in the breeze. "He doesn't have a brain," he says.

Then, just past the entrance to a barn, he will quietly circle a mechanical witch with a pointy hat and bristly broom standing beside a steamy cauldron that she stirs in jerky, repetitive movements with a metal arm mostly concealed by a long black robe. Her face is green and covered with warts. Every few seconds a loud and tinny cackle bursts from the speaker in her throat, and the little boy jumps backward toward the entrance, frightened almost to death. But his father appears out of nowhere, gathers the boy into his arms, hushes him, and dries his wet cheeks against the stubble of his beard before ushering him back toward the pumpkins.

The home video is how I remember the little boy I used to be, here on a family visit to a pumpkin patch when my parents were still married and we all still lived together at the old house. My brother is in diapers as he toddles along beside me while I inspect the pumpkins lined up outside a large red barn, looking for the perfect one to claim as my own. Many of the local farmers just outside our small town would grow fields of pumpkins before Halloween each year and sell them to families to carve and display. Some guarded the steps leading up to modestly decorated front porches, while others glowed in living room windows, candlelight flickering gently from behind the carved-out eyes at night. The farmers would post spray-painted wooden signs alongside the highway pointing down long gravel driveways toward a farmhouse, a red barn, and a pumpkin field set back at a great distance from the road. We must have seen one of those signs on a drive through the winding back roads that day and decided to stop in and take a look. Maybe I had been the one to see the pumpkins from the car window and begged to see them up close.

My grandparents are in the video—in fact, my grandfather is holding the camera, his voice narrating the visit on the camcorder he took everywhere in those days—as well as my uncle, my father's brother. But now when I think of the video, I immediately picture my father and myself. I remember that I make a show of trying to lift up the largest pumpkins, almost as if I'm trying to impress him, sometimes stumbling backward from the effort and causing my father to burst into laughter. Then I grab a handful of gourds stacked around a bale of hay and run toward my father to ask which ones we should take back to arrange on the front porch beside the jack-o'-lantern that I planned to bring alive later that night.

At the end of the video, I'm holding the largest pumpkin I could find that I could still carry on my own as we all amble away from the barn and the rows of pumpkins, back toward the line of cars parked along the gravel driveway leading toward the main road. My face is a mask of concentration as I climb into my father's car, already wondering what kind of expression I want to give the pumpkin. Later, back at home after dark with my mother carefully guiding my hand, I will pick up a knife and begin to carve.

~

I was only six years old when my parents divorced, and my memories of living in what I would later think of as my father's house are like a reel of film haphazardly spliced and reordered, offering only glimpses into the story that took place there. Images from those years float around in my mind unmoored from any narrative function. Flashes of light in an otherwise endless dark.

My mother and father got married just after high school, and a couple years later they moved west from St. Louis across the Missouri River into the first house I remember from my childhood. The neighborhood we lived in had only recently broken ground, just like almost all the others in the suburban town that was rapidly springing up around us. We were the first family to live in the house. The rows and rows of cheap single-story three-bedroom houses with modestly sized yards on streets running parallel to the state highway were popping up like weeds, or so my mother liked to say as we drove past the construction sites in those early days, where bulldozers cleared dirt for the foundations of new houses that would end up looking almost exactly alike. The highway exit at first offered nothing more than a fast-food restaurant and a gas station, a place to stop on the way to somewhere else. But as more and more people moved in, a day care center eventually appeared, then a pharmacy and a small strip mall with a liquor store and a cheap coffee shop. I remember a car repair garage as well, men wiping their faces with dirty rags stuffed casually into the waistbands of their jeans, holes in their shirts where I saw flashes of skin and muscle.

Now, decades later, I can pretend to visit these neighborhoods with the aid of technology, opening an app and clicking somewhere on the streets where my childhood took place, the houses all appearing suddenly on my phone screen as if they'd been folded into a pop-up book for me to open after all these years. I've done this from time to time, and I'm always surprised how difficult it is for me to recognize the house I lived in from all the others on the street, as if it has somehow masked itself over the years, turning into something entirely different from what it had once been.

In my earliest memory from childhood that hasn't been reinforced by videos or photographs, I'm barely five years old and I've been woken up in the middle of the night, alone and afraid. I realize immediately that something is wrong. The fear spreads through my body like electricity as I shake myself more fully awake, and I can already feel the walls of the house creaking around me, the whistle of the wind outside impossibly loud against the window. A storm worse than any I've ever heard. I'm afraid the house will suddenly crumple inward like wet cardboard and smother me in my bed, and when I recall the memory now, I can still hear the voice screaming in my brain, telling me that I have to get up and save my family from whatever has come to destroy us.

Tree branches were flying into the windowpane as I forced myself to place both of my bare feet onto the carpeted floor beside my bed. The lights in the hallway outside my door had gone dark, even the night-light that I insisted always be plugged in. The streetlights that I should have been able to see through the window were out too. My small bedroom had never been so dark before, all those corners now stretching into endless blackness where anything at all could be lying in wait for me.

My mother had always made a point of turning the night-light on after tucking me in, and I knew she wouldn't have allowed it to go out unless something very bad had happened.

I stood up shakily and shuffled into the hallway, my bare toes clinging to the carpet. I called out for my mother, and I heard her say my name from deeper into the house, just as I noticed a flickering light in the direction of the kitchen. I hurried toward the light and turned the corner from the hallway where I saw my mother huddled in front of a single candle at a folding card table—the same table where my father sat while I watched *Halloween* after the rest of us had moved away. She looked small and frightened, like I'd never seen her before. That was when I finally heard the tornado siren, the long high-pitched note of a horn bleating out into the night. To me it was the end of the world. Only then did I allow the tears to come gushing out.

"Come here, come here," my mother said when she saw me standing in the shadows, her arms open wide as I rushed blindly toward her, my vision blurring as the tears continued to fall. She pulled me onto her lap and held me close, drying my cheeks with the palm of her hand. I don't know how long we sat there in the dark together, but I still remember the light of the candle flickering on the table in front of us just past the ashtray, the wax dripping slowly down onto the saucer as I stared at the flame and tried not to listen to the storm raging outside. The smoke from my mother's cigarette swirled in the air, and the candlelight cast dancing shadows on the empty white walls. The house seemed to lean to the side when the tornado passed down our street, but then it righted itself again. The wind died down. The siren stopped wailing. My mother finally sighed deeply, her breath hot against my face.

"It'll be over soon," she whispered, kissing the top of my head. Her fingers holding the cigarette were suddenly trembling. She reached over to snuff out the candle. "It'll all be over soon. Let's get back to bed."

My brother hadn't been woken by the storm, and I somehow knew without having to ask that my father wasn't home. But his absence didn't feel unusual or alarming. I must have already been used to him being gone.

I stood at my bedroom window the next morning, staring blankly at the evidence of destruction on the street outside. Mailboxes had been pulled from the ground and tossed far from the yards where they had been rooted. A neighbor's car was on its side in a pool of shattered glass. We were one of the lucky families whose house remained fully intact, although the gate in the fence alongside the house was gone and several planks had ended up in a neighbor's yard. But that morning my eyes were locked firmly on the house across the street, which had been destroyed by the tornado. The roof had been torn off and the family's furnishings and other belongings were strewn about the yard and down the street. Their kitchen table had broken into two large chunks upon impact after having been lifted up by the ferocious winds, and one chunk was lying in the driveway, splintered and gouged.

No one in the family had been injured because they had fled to their basement at some point during the storm, perhaps after the first of the damage had been done. But I imagined what it must have felt like for them to wander back upstairs after the storm had passed, only to find everything suddenly gone, tossed around and scrambled up and left as scrap in the wake of the storm. What once had been walls and a ceiling was now just empty sky.

I waited for my father to finally make it home from the bar, and I wonder what might have been going through his head as he approached the neighborhood after dozing away his buzz in the parking lot. The hangover from the night before would already have been slicing through his brain as he exited the highway and drove the short distance toward the turnoff to our street, and I wonder if he looked for our cheap furniture among the rubble, maybe for a moment confusing our house with the one that had been destroyed. From my bedroom window I saw his car pull into the driveway and watched him step out unsteadily as he took everything in. Then I heard the front door open and close and my mother's quiet but seething voice as she told him everything that had happened while he was gone.

∼

My father began to add to the house after the tornado, almost as if to weigh it down, to keep it from flying away when the next storm came. He built a deck overlooking the backyard from the garage, painstakingly nailing the wooden planks together on hot weekend afternoons while I watched from the yard. When he was finally finished, he allowed me to help him paint the deck a deep brown color that matched the newly repaired fence that my grandfather had helped him build, and then we stepped back to see what we had made, my father raising his beer can in celebration.

That winter a massive snowstorm made the roads impassable for days, canceled school, and had us all pacing around the house while we waited to dig ourselves out. My father showed me how to build an igloo from the snow that had gathered on the deck. I would hide away inside its thickly packed walls for as long as I could bear the cold, my brother having gone back inside the house long before I did, his face red from crying when I told him we would have to cut off his hands and feet if he didn't warm them up soon and hypothermia set in. I stayed inside the igloo until my fingers turned blue and I couldn't stop my body from shaking, believing I could learn to withstand the cold if only I suffered it long enough. The next summer my father installed an above-ground swimming pool in the backyard—not long before my mother, brother, and I moved away—and my parents threw weekend parties for the neighbors, who drank beers on the deck while my brother and I swam around with the other children down in the yard.

My brother wore giant inflatable wings around his arms while I held his hand and dragged him through the water. The older boys would be splashing the girls, who only pretended not to like it, screeching and squealing and squirming away from the boys' touch in their flimsy bikinis, exposing skin that I could tell, without fully understanding why, was driving the boys crazy. I would hold my breath and sink underwater with my goggles suctioned to my face to watch all of their bare legs jumping and kicking in slow motion in what was almost like a dance when seen from below.

I remember a game we played in which we all kept to the edge of the pool while kicking as hard as we could in a circle to make a whirlpool current. Then we would let our bodies relax and allow the water to propel us forward while we floated on our backs, staring up at the bright blue sky as we were pulled round and round by the force we had generated.

～

Another memory, from later that summer. My brother and I are in the back seat of my mother's car late at night, and we've stopped at the scene of an accident. We're alone. I must have been asleep before that moment, because my eyes fly open and I see police cars and ambulances on the road in front of us, the view from the car window all flashing lights and swirling orbs in the otherwise infinite darkness. A sense of danger pushes away any thoughts of falling asleep again. I don't know where I am and I don't remember being woken up in my bed, or at least that part of the memory is gone. I can hear my mother's voice through the open window, and then I see that she's talking to a police officer holding a notepad and speaking occasionally into a walkie-talkie. Her hands gesture wildly in the air.

Two lanes of the highway have been blocked off, and cars in the other lanes creep by slowly while drivers take in what has happened, maybe wondering about the amount of damage and whether anyone has been seriously hurt. I reach up and pull myself forward with the headrest of the driver's seat in front of me, and that's when I see my father's car completely destroyed and in pieces all across the pavement in front of us, just past the police tape and the ambulance and an empty stretcher. I recognize the license plate still attached to the broken bumper, but I don't see my father anywhere.

My mother must have woken us immediately after getting the call. We were still too young to be left alone even for an emergency like this one, so she had to take us with her to the scene of the accident. When she climbs back into the car, she doesn't tell us right away what has happened. "Your dad is okay," she says, looking into the rearview mirror as she backs up the car. She meets my eyes briefly and then glances over at my brother who has already fallen back asleep beside me.

My father had been driving back from the bar when he fell asleep behind the wheel and drove into the guardrail along the interstate. He'd been so drunk that he didn't even have the instinct to press on the brakes, and the car had skidded along before finally flipping onto its side. The ambulance had already swallowed him up by the time we got there, and I didn't see him at all that night.

I've always remembered that my father's left arm was twisted unnaturally at the elbow after recovering from the accident, the fingers on his curled hand gnarled and bent due to the injuries he'd sustained. But my mother now tells me that his arm had been like that because of another accident, years before I was born, when he had been drinking and while my mother was also in the car. I've somehow created a before-and-after in my mind, but she says I never actually saw him without the injury—that it had been a part of him for as long as I'd known him—

which came as a shock when I recounted the memory to her and was corrected by her own account, so clearly did I remember his transformation. But the accident I've described must have been some other night, some other wreckage. My mother says that she and my father had been driving home with the windows down from a party at a friend's house when the first accident took place, newly married teenagers imagining the future before them like a summer that would never end. She says that the wreck was the end of something for her, but also a harbinger of things to come. And when I think now of my father's left hand, I picture it bent and twisted but still clutching a beer can, the aluminum gently crinkled from where he grasped it between his otherwise useless fingers.

I'd thought for so long that I'd seen as a child the aftermath of the accident that had made him that way. I was so sure it was that night of bright lights and broken glass that had done it.

~

In my last memory of living in my father's house, I've just turned six years old, and I wake up once again in the middle of the night. The streets outside my window are dark and empty. I hear my mother crying out from the kitchen, and then my father's voice, unnaturally loud, the language garbled and angry.

My heart began racing even as I shook the sleep away. I'd heard my parents fighting before, usually when my father hadn't come home until long after dark. He hadn't been home when I'd gone to bed that night, but I didn't register that as strange, just the way things had always been. But now there was the sound of something crashing to the kitchen floor, then shattering. Something fragile and made of glass. My mother howled like a cornered animal, one long sob from deep inside her body. The arguments I'd heard before had always been heated but hushed, as if the violence between them was some kind of secret. But this was different. She needed someone to hear. I threw off the sheets and ran down the same hallway I'd cautiously stepped through on the night of the tornado, and when I turned the corner and entered the small kitchen I saw my mother cowering against the card table, bent at the waist as she leaned over and turned her body desperately away from my father.

He loomed large above her in that moment, even though he was actually a few inches shorter than she was. Broken glass was scattered across the tiled floor, and I realized my father must have thrown something at

38

my mother. Maybe a drinking glass or a beer bottle or the large ashtray in the center of the table that was always filled to the brim with cigarette butts. No one had seen me yet, my bare feet still pressed into the carpet at the threshold between the hallway and the kitchen. My mother couldn't see past the hands that she kept up to hide her face, her sobs muffled behind her fingers, and my father was standing with his back to me as he scrambled to pull my mother up to him, his one good hand already in a fist.

I don't know if I made a sound when I ran toward them, but suddenly I was standing in front of my mother trying to block her from my father, facing him down as I thought a man was supposed to do. I was trying to make everything stop. The words coming out of my father's mouth were incoherent but loud, his face red and angry in a way that also seemed unfocused and confused, as if he'd already forgotten what it was that had upset him in the first place. And the blow my father had intended for my mother stopped just short of my own face, his hand a closed fist floating before me like something coming down from the sky, from outer space—from somewhere none of us had ever been.

I instinctively folded myself into my mother's arms as my father stumbled backward in the other direction, blinking away his confusion and then silently walking back to the bedroom at the end of the hallway that he'd shared with my mother until that night when everything changed forever. The last thing I remember is my knees buckling and landing hard on the kitchen floor just after my father went away, the tiles cold on my skin through my thin pajamas, pain searing up through my body as my bones ground against the cheap tile. My mother continuing to sob, her face now buried in my neck, arms tight around my chest and back as if I would float away if she ever let me go.

4

We moved out of the old house soon after that night. My father stayed at a motel until we were gone.

I remember urgent phone conversations as my mother arranged for us to move—with help from my grandparents—into a narrow townhouse in a new housing complex just down the main road from where we had lived with my father. Another cheap new neighborhood popping up out of nowhere. The long rows of connected alternating white and brick townhouses stretched back from the turnoff past a small fire station in what had once been an open field of overgrown grass. My brother and I had sometimes run through it in the summertime with other kids from the old neighborhood, getting lost in the sea of green and then following each other's voices all the way back home.

I didn't yet understand exactly what was happening when we visited the empty model townhouse for the first time, my brother and I racing up the stairs excitedly—we had never lived in a house with two floors before—and beginning to stake claim to our own sides of the large bedroom we would share for the next several years, a bunk bed in the center to mark the boundaries of our separate spaces. I didn't understand yet that my father wasn't going to be moving there with us. I didn't know it was possible for us to leave him behind.

I hadn't seen him since the day of the move, when he showed up unannounced one weekend afternoon while we were still unpacking boxes. The divorce must have been almost finalized by then, the custody arrangements still being sorted out. When my mother answered the knock at the door, I was sitting on the new living room couch reading a book that I quietly set aside when I saw my father standing there. She went outside to the porch, and I could hear their muffled voices through the wall, my father quietly pleading with her for us to come back home. But my mother's voice was stern and sharp in her response to everything he had to say.

I watched the sky change through the window while I pieced together the words I could catch. My father said he would do better. He would be at home more often. He would make everything right. But I knew when my mother came inside that we wouldn't be going back, even though she had tears on her cheeks when she quietly closed the door behind her. My father caught my eye just as it clicked shut. I made my face look angry when he saw me, remembering the night in the kitchen, how close he'd come to striking me.

Over the several years that followed, my brother and I would go back and forth between our mother's and our father's houses on the weekends, the distance between them less than a mile of state road. Between them were a small church and a gas station where I would buy soda and snacks with coins I dumped out from the pint glass on my father's dresser, and sometimes I'd steal the candy I liked when there were no coins to take. There was also a dense line of trees running alongside a dry creek bed separating the two neighborhoods, and I would sometimes hide in those woods for hours on end, hunting for frogs and snakes that I'd trap in glass jars looted from trash bins left out at the ends of driveways. I would build forts in clearings that I carefully swept clean of rocks and fallen branches, mapping the boundaries of my secret kingdom as I kept everyone else out.

I invited my brother to join me in the woods only once. I was probably around seven or eight years old at the time, so he would have been four or five. He was always following me around everywhere I went, so I knew he'd someday discover where I'd been hiding. But I didn't want him there. I didn't want him to know how to find me. One day I told him I had a secret to share with him, and we stepped from a neighbor's backyard into the trees. I knew the way to the area I'd most recently cleared, but I didn't want him to see it. We went in the other direction. I walked ahead of him until we couldn't see the path anymore, and I told him to close his eyes and count to ten. Then I quietly stepped away from him and hid behind a tree.

He was calling my name before he'd even finished counting, so he must have opened his eyes and seen that I had disappeared.

I pressed my palm against my mouth to keep from laughing as I heard his frightened, childish cries turn to heaving sobs, anything he was saying now completely incomprehensible to anyone who might have been listening. When I finally stole a glance at him from behind the tree, I saw that he had squatted down on the ground in the fallen leaves with his eyes closed, covering his face with his hands. He heard a branch snap as I took a step toward him, and when his face whirled around toward the sound—his eyes already swimming with tears—I saw in his horrified expression that he had expected to see some kind of monster coming for him, a troll who waited in the woods for little boys to eat, the big bad wolf in disguise. But it was only me.

"Why were you hiding from me?" he asked. His voice was small, almost swallowed up by the woods around us. "You didn't say it was a game."

"I wasn't hiding," I said. "It wasn't a game. The trees made me disappear. Never come back here because the trees might make you disappear too. We might never see you again."

I made a noise like a roar and chased him all the way back home.

From then on, the woods between my mother's and my father's houses were my own secret domain. I could see the outer edges of both neighborhoods through gaps in the trees, the familiar houses and parked cars reminding me I'd need to head back home again before dark. But when the leaves were thickest and I was completely concealed from anyone who might have been looking for me, I could imagine I'd actually gone miles and miles away, even perhaps having crossed over into another world. I wanted the woods to be enchanted. I wanted to encounter magical creatures that would send me on a perilous quest from which I might never return. I wanted to stumble upon the wolf in disguise and to escape from his jaws when he tried to gobble me up. I wanted to get lost in the dark and then be rescued by a hero who had been searching tirelessly for me all along.

Sometimes I would go into the woods at night after everyone else was asleep. I'd move slowly and aimlessly through the trees, my hands grazing the low-hanging branches as I tried to keep myself from tumbling into a ravine or slipping on a pile of wet leaves that would send me careening down a hill. Then later I'd sneak back into the house as quietly as possible, locking the door behind me before climbing the stairs back up to the bedroom I shared with my brother. One night he was awake on the bottom bunk when I returned from the woods. He was sitting upright and staring directly toward the doorway when I walked in from the dark hallway, his shaggy brown hair messy and tangled from sleep.

"Where'd you go?" he asked.

He looked like he'd been crying, but he hadn't woken our mother. He must have heard me leave. He must have waited this whole time to see whether I would be coming back. He clasped his hands together on his lap, leaning forward into the streetlight glow streaming in through the thin curtain as he waited for me to answer.

"Nowhere," I finally said. But there were leaves clinging to the sleeves of my sweatshirt, brambles lodged into the fabric of my jeans. My brother looked down at my feet where my wet socks had darkened the green carpet. I smelled like the woods. I must have looked as if I'd been running away from something chasing me through the night, frantic and afraid, and had only now made it back home to safety.

I climbed up the ladder to my own bed, the sheets still tucked in around the edges of the mattress and my pillow still dented from where I'd waited earlier until I thought my brother was asleep before venturing out. "Go back to sleep," I said. "It'll be morning soon."

Then I closed my eyes and was soon in the dream about the long hallway. I could see the man at the end of it, waiting for me in the distance, a dark outline in the ceaseless gray shadows. I was getting closer and closer. It was only a matter of time.

∼

Alone now in the old house without my mother there to take care of things, my father was slipping further and further into his own world, the objects that had once made it a home slowly falling away into disrepair or rot. We'd left almost everything behind when we moved away, buying all new furniture on clearance at the outlet store off the highway: the lacquered dropleaf table we shoved into the small dining area at the townhouse, the cheap living room couch directly from the showroom floor that was marked down because its cushions had already begun to fray. But the furniture and household items we'd left behind in my father's house quickly became broken or neglected to the point of ruin.

The microwave no longer worked. Mysterious stains appeared on the couch and the armchair by the window where he often sat. Plastic ashtrays full of cigarette butts completely covered the coffee table. The refrigerator was always empty except for my father's beer.

My brother and I never slept over during our Saturday visits. The house no longer felt like ours. Most of the evidence that children had once lived there was gone, and we would bring things to entertain ourselves while our father dipped in and out of naps, sleeping off the morning's beers before starting up again in the afternoon in front of the kitchen TV. I brought my paperback books, always horror, anything I could read fast with my heart thudding loud in my chest. And then later, after the trip to the video store with my father, I finally had Michael to keep me company.

My first glimpse of Haddonfield in *Halloween* aside from the view of the Myers house in the opening flashback sequence was of a quiet intersection in a peaceful neighborhood with newly bare trees along the sidewalk, autumn leaves strewn across the pavement. But just before that, I watched Michael escape from the asylum. The escape narrative is what sets the action of the film in motion.

The outskirts of the asylum loom in the darkness as Dr. Loomis, Michael's psychiatrist for the past fifteen years, and a nurse drive up to the gates in a thunderstorm, headlights scanning the rain-slicked road before them. Then the eerie soundtrack is cued as Loomis notices several patients aimlessly wandering the grounds on the other side of a short fence. While the nurse expresses befuddlement, Loomis immediately suspects foul play and races from the car toward an intercom at the gate leading to the hospital grounds, just as Michael himself appears out of nowhere in the car's rearview mirror. He manages to leap onto the car and then somehow into it, a sequence that largely defies logic. The nurse has been cast out onto the ground on her hands and knees, and I remember the thrill of watching Michael drive away in the stolen car, everything that could now happen because he was free—all the different places he could go, even if in the end he only wanted to make his way back home.

I was having my own fantasies of escape at the time. I wanted to become someone else, to carve out a new identity for myself. I imagined somehow changing my body and my face, coming up with a new name and arriving in some other town with a story about myself different from the one I'd been given. The fantasy of escape often involved hitching a ride with a stranger by standing on a corner of the state road outside the housing complex with my thumb held high. The driver of the car that picked me up was always a man, and he was always alone, sometimes smoking a cigarette or sipping from a can of beer. I would ride with him as far as he would take me, sneaking glances at him while he drove, and when he caught me looking, he would smile sideways at me while still keeping an eye on the road, the corner of his lip drifting up into his dimpled cheek.

These fantasies also often involved imaginary worlds of my own creation, magical places where I would have secret knowledge about how to traverse the landscape or unlock a door where treasures awaited me. And of course these were worlds where I would be imbued with special powers. The power to read minds. The ability to fly. Invisibility. This last superpower was particularly alluring to me because I was interested in having access to spaces where I was not otherwise allowed to be, or to openly watch something I would otherwise have had to pretend not to be interested in. Something I shouldn't actually want.

I remember weekend visits to the pool in town when I would bashfully change into my swimsuit in an empty corner of the locker room before later making every possible excuse to go back there afterward from the pool, pretending to be fumbling with my locker combination while glancing over at the older boys as they flaunted their wet and muscled bodies, completely unaware of the power they held over me. How they could have made me do anything they wanted just by asking. But the pleasure of looking was always undermined by the fear of being found out, and I always knew that the objects of my desire must not in any way be made plain.

One summer there was a lifeguard I watched every chance I could get, begging my mother to take me to the pool on the weekends just so I could see his lightly freckled skin glistening with sweat in the late afternoon sun. Girls dawdled at the base of the ladder leading up to his perch and giggled as they tried to make him look their way. The girls could watch him openly, harmlessly, but I had to watch from a distance. I had to pretend to not be watching him at all. But I can still picture him, the way his sunglasses reflected everything back at me—

the pool beneath the lifeguard stand, the sunbathers on their lounge chairs, small children splashing in the shallows—like some kind of movie projection. I liked that I couldn't tell exactly where his gaze would linger. I liked pretending he was watching only me, our eyes meeting across the crowded pool. I liked imagining how it would feel for him to sweep me up into his arms and whisk me away to a place where no one could find us.

I might have been wondering at the time how long Michael Myers had been planning his escape from the asylum, waiting for the perfect moment to disappear into the night, the taillights of the stolen car growing fainter and fainter in the distance until there was no evidence of him ever having been there at all.

~

The magical exists alongside the everyday in fairy tales, infecting the known world with the fantastic and the unexplainable. Michael Myers shouldn't be able to disappear from view so quickly during his early pursuit of Laurie Strode through the streets of Haddonfield, his masked face briefly glimpsed by her through a classroom window and then later in his black coveralls in the backyard among clothes hung out to dry. And yet he does. He shouldn't be able to watch her from what seem to be multiple vantage points at once, his off-screen body moving through space so much more seamlessly than when he's actually in the frame. And yet he does.

The only body *not* projected onto the screen in a horror film is that of the spectator, and in this way the film becomes a mirror. After that first viewing at my father's house, during which he eventually disappeared into his bedroom to sleep off the effects of the beers he'd been drinking steadily throughout the day, I became wholly obsessed with the world of Haddonfield. Michael had appeared just when I needed him most, falling in step beside me as I walked toward whatever fate awaited me. The film's ominous score quickly became the soundtrack to my own life, and I would hum its simple notes as I walked or cycled through the neighborhood streets. By then our small town had become for me a direct facsimile of Haddonfield, where Michael's future victims sauntered home from school on sidewalks shaded by autumn leaves, clutching textbooks and discussing their plans for the night—jack-o'-lanterns to carve, scary movies to watch, boys to kiss behind closed doors in dark bedrooms—unaware of the nightmare that awaited them as soon as darkness fell.

Halloween seemed interested in casting light into the shadows of seemingly recognizable settings that otherwise might not attract a second glance—deceptively familiar places we thought we understood, but had in fact deeply underestimated. I relished most the scenes in which Michael appeared almost out of nowhere, always unexpectedly, as if he were actually everywhere at once and just waiting patiently for the right moment to reveal himself—or disappear into thin air when Laurie noticed he was watching her. I was entranced by the way he moved so slowly and ploddingly down the quiet sidewalks and across those dark suburban lawns, knife in hand and white mask firmly attached to his face. Yet he always managed to catch up to the young people who would soon become his victims, as if the act of being deliberate about his choices was enough for him to get exactly what he wanted.

The camera adopts not only the pace of Michael's frighteningly methodical gait, but also the nature of his singular perspective. Exterior shots of seemingly mundane suburban streets are framed as if viewed not by an audience but by a bystander, someone watching unnoticed just off to the side of its characters' immediate perspective. The film teaches a voyeuristic way of being in the world, a way of looking without being seen. And in that way I recognized myself as its student.

~

I finally stopped watching *Halloween* on a continuous loop when my brother and I stopped going inside my father's house at all during our visits. My portal to Haddonfield remained forever on the other side of a doorway through which I had come to dread passing.

My father's eyes were always glassy and far away by then. Empty beer cans littered every surface of the kitchen, the carpet in the hallway perpetually soiled from his failed attempts to make it to the bathroom before being sick. My mother no longer went inside the house when she dropped us off. For all we knew, the two of them hadn't spoken in a very long time. I don't think my father even knew what day it was most of the time, and therefore he wouldn't have known when to expect us. Cockroaches had colonized his kitchen and then spread farther when he made no attempt to banish them, crawling up and down the walls and gathering in terrifying herds in the bathtub and the sink. He would pass out either on the couch or in his bed and then wake up and start drinking again.

Most of the time I couldn't understand the words he was saying to me. Most of the time I didn't even try.

My mother would drop us off outside his house on Saturday mornings during the last summer he lived there—the summer I turned twelve. Sometimes she gave us money for the ice cream truck before saying goodbye and driving off. Then we stored the small blue cooler containing our lunches in the back seat of his car, which was parked in the driveway and never locked because one of the windows had somehow been shattered and replaced with only a thin sheet of plastic where the glass had been. We held our breath so as not to be overwhelmed by the smell inside the car, trying to ignore the mysterious stains on the upholstery. Then we spent the day playing with the neighborhood kids we knew from when we'd still lived there.

A girl named B, who was just one year ahead of me in school, lived next door. Her two brothers were usually spending time with their girlfriends or driving their father's car around the neighborhood and smoking cigarettes. Sometimes she and I would hang out in her basement, where she had an air hockey table and a dartboard with real darts, not like the plastic ones at the day care center. I would throw the darts at the wall as hard as I could and watch them get lodged at odd angles in the plaster, pretending I'd missed the board by accident when B was watching. I liked the holes in the wall that the darts left behind. She usually had music playing on the small radio on a metal shelf by the window, the local pop station coming in fuzzy but loud, and sometimes she would dance like crazy through the basement to a particular song she liked, her hands in the air pulling down cobwebs from the rafters that would cling to her long blond hair and trail behind her like a cape as she spun through the shadows.

One day we were down in B's basement as usual, just the two of us sitting on a beige rug laid out over the concrete where we'd spent long afternoons playing poker with pennies she poured out of a large glass jar. I'd left my brother out by the sidewalk with a few other kids where he was creating an elaborate hopscotch game on the concrete with thick pieces of chalk. B had switched on the skinny lamp that leaned against the wall. Its extension cord stretched toward a plug across the basement from where we were sitting. The base of the lamp cast a long shadow.

"I have a surprise for you," she said, her voice almost a whisper as she leaned forward on her knees. She grinned like she was about to break some kind of rule, and I pressed my hands into the carpet on either side of my crossed legs, wondering what she was about to give me. Maybe one of the sour candies she knew I liked. Or maybe she'd found a new game for us to play. But before I could prepare myself for what she had in store for me, she had hooked her thumbs around the hem of her T-shirt and pulled it up to expose her pierced navel, the slope of her belly, and then even farther to reveal her bare breasts, the flesh of them drooping just below her ribcage as she leaned closer and closer to me across the rug, her nipples pointed down to the ground.

Maybe this was something she was giving me just this once, something that might bring me closer to being a man. But I threw myself backward in a sudden panic. I couldn't get away fast enough. The room almost seemed to spin around me as she pulled her shirt back down again, squirming and giggling as she rocked back and forth on her knees.

"You should see your face," she said, but I was already scrambling up the stairs.

I avoided her during visits to the neighborhood after that afternoon, hiding from whatever she wanted me to see. I would leave my brother with his friends and wander the neighborhood streets alone, peering into the windows of houses and imagining what kinds of lives happened inside each of them. I was thinking about Haddonfield: danger lurking behind every hedgerow, the possibility of the bogeyman stepping out onto the sidewalk in front of me and the knowledge that he would be able to catch me no matter how fast I ran in the opposite direction. Sometimes I even pretended at being Laurie, alone and pursued and in danger, always looking over my shoulder.

T's murder the following spring would send me back to these long afternoons alone, picturing all the other ways it could have gone. I'd think back and our faces would blend together into a composite of defenselessness, both of us resigned to whatever was coming for us. The car moving slowly toward me down the street was being driven by someone who would kidnap me and take me away forever. The empty backyards I wandered through were actually not empty at all, and someone was waiting to jump out at me from behind every toolshed or every parked car, knife already in hand. Maybe he would even be wearing a mask.

Sometimes I hid beneath open windows and listened to the intimate conversations that took place between adults while their children were outside playing. I spied on backyard barbecues from behind trees and wooden fences, and I once spent an entire afternoon swimming in the pool in a neighbor's backyard, flipping a latch and walking right through the gate. I knew I was safe because I'd watched the family leave that morning in a minivan packed with luggage for a family vacation. The sunburn that resulted from my surreptitious day of floating and paddling around in direct sunlight left my skin itchy and tight for days.

One afternoon I ventured too close to a birthday party for a boy around my age, and before I knew it, someone's mother had fastened a birthday hat to my head and handed me a piece of cake on a paper plate. I played games with these strangers all day, eating their treats and drinking soda from a cooler in the shade. I even took my turn at a piñata, the blindfold tight against my face as I wildly swung the bat, everyone cheering me on from the sidelines as the candy finally whooshed out onto the ground, all the other kids scrambling to grab their share.

No one ever knew I hadn't been invited.

5

I LIKED PRETENDING TO BE LAURIE STRODE on those long Saturdays spent walking around my father's neighborhood, even though I suspected no one was actually following me down the street and making plans for what he'd do when he finally caught me. No one was lurking behind me and ducking out of sight each time I looked over my shoulder. No one was tracking my movements, waiting for darkness to fall before he finally made his move. No one was interested in me at all. But I thought Laurie was beautiful, and I wanted to be beautiful. I wanted someone to see me walking alone on the sidewalk and realize that he had to have me no matter what it would take. He wouldn't stop until he had me in his arms. I wanted to be something that someone desired so badly that he would kill to get it.

When I first saw Laurie walking out the door of her white suburban house carrying a stack of textbooks on her way to school, I saw what I imagined my mother had looked like as a teenager. The same hair, a light auburn color with long bangs rolled slightly at the bottom edges so that they turned out like wings. Laurie had most likely sat at a vanity table like my mother's earlier that morning, running her hair through a curling iron to make it look just right. Now outside, she walks quickly across the quiet street and sees Tommy Doyle—the little boy she'll be babysitting later that evening—running toward her. He's wearing jeans and a light jacket like the one I'd worn at the pumpkin patch in the home video with my father, blond hair hanging over his ears as he talks excitedly about what activities they'll be doing together later on that Halloween night. Carve a jack-o'-lantern. Watch a monster movie. Make popcorn. And when I first saw them crossing the street together, I realized with a jolt that I was looking at my mother and myself.

Later in the film, while babysitting Tommy at his house as night takes hold of Haddonfield, Laurie peers out the window at the steadily darkening neighborhood and whispers to herself, "Everybody's having a good time tonight." She believes she's the only one who isn't, conscripted to parental duties rather than being allowed to experience the wild abandon of adolescence for herself. I remember my mother home each night during those first years after the divorce, rather than out with friends or on dates. Only when she started working at the bar did she begin to make friends and meet new men like the one who had followed her home on that terrifying night and then the one I later saw almost naked in the hallway, irrevocably igniting my imagination. She spent birthdays alone, downstairs in the townhouse at the dining room table, drinking cheap pink wine dispensed from a box. Most nights she stayed up late, reading a book or a magazine until she fell asleep on the recliner in the living room, the upholstery later riddled with burn marks when she failed to put out her cigarette before nodding off.

Sometimes when I couldn't sleep I'd climb down from the top bunk and shuffle quietly to the staircase in my pajamas to watch her from the shadows behind the railing, my back pressed to the wall and my eyes stinging from the cigarette smoke swirling through the air below. One night I heard her voice from where I stood at the top of the stairs and I froze in place, worried I'd been found out. Then I realized she was only talking to someone on the phone.

I descended a few steps so I could hear her more clearly, and I sat down quietly in my usual spot where I could see my mother through the slats of the railing. She was sitting on the farthest edge of the couch, close to the wall where the phone was plugged into the jack. She wore a long white nightgown that I knew was torn on the sleeve, twirling the phone cord absently between her fingers and dropping it occasionally to take a drag of the cigarette resting in the ashtray on the cushion beside her.

"I'm worried," she said. "He keeps so much to himself. Not like he doesn't talk to me, because we definitely talk. He likes to talk about his books. That's why I couldn't take them away from him, even though his teacher wanted me to. She said it was inappropriate, a little kid reading about those sorts of things. Can you believe it? At least he's reading. He just loves to be scared, I guess. And that *Halloween* movie he loves so much . . ."

My face went hot and for a moment I couldn't see clearly. I felt as if my skin had been peeled away and now I was just a fragile skeleton, nothing left to keep all the parts of me intact. My mother took a long drag of her cigarette, and I heard a muffled voice on the other end of the line in the dead quiet of the living room. A woman's voice consoling my mother, maybe a friend from the bar whom she usually talked to while pouring beers from the tap or wiping the insides of newly rinsed pint glasses with a dishrag after all the customers had gone home.

"I can't believe he's going to be in middle school next year," my mother said finally. "It's all happening so fast."

A thin, cheap beige blanket was draped over her shoulders and pulled tightly around her chest. We couldn't afford to heat the house properly during the winter, so we all wore layer upon layer of clothing while at home, sweatshirts and long underwear and hoodies, swaddling ourselves in thick blankets at night in our beds. I realized I was shivering in my pajamas, which were already too short at the ankle after I'd grown two inches seemingly overnight, and I pulled my knees to my chest to make myself as small as possible, trying to keep all the heat inside.

My mother laughed suddenly at something the woman on the other end of the line had said. "I know, I know," she said. "I just want him to fit in. To be like the other boys."

How dare she talk about me like that, I thought. I wanted to run down into the living room yelling at the top of my voice to make her see how wrong she was about me. What she thought was loneliness was instead a rage I'd been nurturing in secret, something alive inside me getting stronger and stronger, waiting for the perfect time to make itself known. I gripped the railing of the staircase so hard that I thought the wood might splinter beneath my fingers, the whole house coming apart around me.

Another drag from the cigarette, the flame near her fingertips brightening as she inhaled. The bulb in the lamp beside her on the end table flickered.

"He must feel so alone," she said.

~

While walking around my old neighborhood on those weekly visits to my father's house, I recalled how Haddonfield looked through the windows

53

of Michael's stolen car as dusk fell on Halloween night and he drove slowly through the streets, no one inside all those houses set back from the tree-lined sidewalks aware that he was watching. That he was hunting. I would sneak sidelong glances at the older boys mowing lawns or working on their cars, always shirtless and tanned and greasy, summertime sweat gliding down their muscled backs and onto the rags dangling from their waists for wiping the moisture from their foreheads as they squinted into the bright sunlight.

Sometimes I would even follow them—groups of boys walking together, teasing each other with punches and jabs at the ribs, dribbling a basketball or riding skateboards alongside each other and kicking up here and there on a single set of wheels as I'd seen other boys do in movies. Or sometimes I'd watch just one boy listening to music on headphones attached to a Walkman on his way to another boy's house to play video games, and I would get as close to him as possible, testing the limits of my ability to remain unseen.

I didn't yet have the words to describe what I knew I was doing by looking, but years later I enrolled in a horror film seminar in college, and the assigned readings finally gave me language for the experience I'd internalized when I first saw Michael stalking his victims. The sadism of the voyeur. The spectator as a Peeping Tom. The ruthless, brutal thrills of watching. Horror as a reenactment of the repressed. The professor discussed the attacker and the attacked in the horror film as two parts of the same self, the viewer positioned as both hunter and hunted, depending on the perspective of the camera. In a horror film, the act of looking can kill.

Michael doesn't turn his gaze upon Laurie for nothing, after all. But the boys in my old neighborhood didn't know I was watching them, or else they simply didn't make anything of it. I was just a little kid in a blue dinosaur T-shirt and red shorts walking slowly along the curb, my sneakers buckled with Velcro. Those boys probably wouldn't have given me a second glance if they'd even noticed me at all. And I already knew what they would do to me if they knew what I really wanted from them. Fists pummeling my face, fast kicks to my chest once they'd thrown me down. I would see the faces of these beautiful boys through the blood and the tears streaming down my face, watching them laugh as my vision blurred until I couldn't see anything at all.

In Haddonfield, Tommy Doyle knows from the beginning that the bogeyman has arrived, but no one takes him seriously until it's much too late. He's bullied by a group of older boys at the end of the school day as other children already in their Halloween costumes stream chaotically out the front doors of the elementary school, clowns and cowboys and ballerinas chattering excitedly as the bell rings through the air around them. Tommy is walking slowly down a shadowed hallway, holding a pumpkin almost too large for him to carry on his own, and he's being closely followed by three bigger boys crowding in from behind. "Look at your stupid pumpkin," one of them says. Tommy finally turns around to defend himself, and the boys begin chanting about the bogeyman. "He's gonna get you, he's gonna get you," the boys repeat as they surround Tommy threateningly. He finally breaks free only to trip over an outstretched sneaker and crumple to the ground, the pumpkin transformed into a pulpy mess beneath the weight of his small body.

By the time I saw Tommy for the first time, I'd already lost several friends who had gotten too close to seeing what I was, friends who had once been kind but then suddenly began to avoid me, perhaps already understanding the ways in which we might be different. I would go on sleepovers and attend birthday parties but never be invited back. I saw in the faces of the other boys that I always did something wrong. I wouldn't know the rules of the games I was forced to play, or I would be made to pretend I had an interest in certain kinds of toys, but something always gave me away. The pitch of my laughter when we watched a movie together, or the way I would shy away from physical contact. One boy tried to wrestle with me at a basement slumber party, and I didn't know where to put my hands on his body—and whether I had even wanted to free myself of his grip as he pinned me to the ground, how good it felt to be powerless against the weight of him.

But then there was a boy who approached me on the school playground one day during recess. I'd been walking the perimeter of the railroad ties separating the gravel from the concrete and daring myself not to fall to either side. He'd been doing the same thing, and we met somewhere in the middle. He caught my eye and didn't look away. We decided to make a game out of it, seeing who could walk the farthest without stumbling to the side. He was in another class, but I'd seen him on the playground before—usually alone like me, keeping away from the rowdier games that the other boys played. Freckles like a swath of brown paint crossed his round cheeks, his straight hair sometimes tangled at his ears. We started meeting at the playground every day, and then he invited me to join him one weekend at the arcade in the lobby of the movie theater in the next town over. His mother picked me up where I was waiting excitedly on the front porch of the townhouse, and we played Ping-Pong and a NASCAR racing game all afternoon until she came to take us home after seeing a movie with a friend. Then we started hanging out every weekend, either going to the arcade or seeing a movie or playing video games in his bedroom, just the two of us alone together for hours.

I would always see him across the playground when I ran through the double doors with the other kids in my class, his eyes searching for me in the pack. His eagerness for my company became painfully obvious, and it was probably in one of those moments that I knew. The relief that flooded his body when he saw me, the smile that would erupt across his face as I walked toward him.

Over time I grew to find his neediness repulsive. He was allergic to various foods, and he was often sick with a cold, constantly sniffling and wiping his nose with the back of his hand. One Saturday afternoon while we were playing a new video game at his house that I'd brought over, I felt his elbow pressed against mine as he leaned into a demanding series of maneuvers. He didn't move his arm even after the match was over, and something in the way our bodies were touching made me feel exposed and vulnerable, the pressure of his body against mine telling me something about what he might want from me. I suddenly found myself calling him disgusting and repulsive, using words that other boys would have said if they'd seen us together like that. I threw down my game controller and mocked him cruelly, sneering as I vigorously wiped my hand against my nose in a cruel imitation of his own frequent gesture. I told him I didn't want to hold the game controllers anymore because then I would catch whatever it was he had. And then I stomped down the stairs and demanded that his mother drive me home.

He had followed behind me and was standing on the front porch as his mother backed down the driveway. I fumbled with my seatbelt in the back seat, squirming at the memory of what I'd said to him—the shocked look on his face when he realized how badly I'd wanted to hurt him. He didn't wave goodbye, just stood there with his arms hanging at his sides. He never waited for me at the playground again, but I would have looked away if I'd seen his eyes on me. And I would have pretended not to hear his voice if he'd ever called my name from where he was always standing alone near the swings, kicking gravel around at his feet and squinting with his hand to his forehead to shield his eyes from the glare of the sun.

I didn't want this boy to feel safe in my company. I didn't want anyone to see us together and think we were the same.

∽

In the end, I watched one boy in particular on those long Saturday walks while I waited for my mother to come and pick us up from the old neighborhood. He lived on the same block as my father, but his house was farther from the turnoff to the main road, all the way down at the end of the long line of single-story houses. He was older than me, probably already in high school when I first noticed him—blond hair that he kept tucked behind his ears and a long, lean torso, cutoff shorts he wore a couple inches too big at the waist always sagging below his hips past a flash of white underwear clinging tight against his skin.

My breath caught in my throat when I saw him for the first time. He was lazily kicking a soccer ball on the hot pavement of the sidewalk outside my father's house, bare-chested with a white T-shirt tied around his waist and traces of sunburn pinkening his shoulders. I'd been eating lunch with my brother in the shade between my father's house and the house next door, trying to avoid the blazing heat of the summer day, but I abandoned my sandwich and walked slowly away from my brother when I saw this boy pass by, almost as if I'd been hypnotized. I began to follow him, keeping a few house lengths back at first, watching his taut legs move side to side in response to wherever the soccer ball had ended up ahead of him. The ball sometimes darted into a neighbor's yard or threatened to roll into the street before he expertly regained control with quick reflexes and subtle movements of his feet, but then it ended up lodged beneath a car parked at the end of a driveway and blocking the sidewalk. I heard him curse loudly as he awkwardly maneuvered his leg beneath the car, finally retrieving the ball. Then he suddenly turned around and looked right at me.

He must have seen my reflection in the car window and realized he was being followed, and he met my eyes just as I turned away from his

57

gaze. I had to pretend that I'd arrived at my own house, when in fact the ugly beige house I was standing in front of belonged to a family of strangers. I walked slowly up the driveway toward the front door, afraid of what he would say to me if someone came out and told me to go away, revealing the truth of what I'd been doing. I pictured the sneer that would darken his otherwise beautiful face, the way his body would unspool with rage. But when I took my first step onto the front porch and dared a quick glance over my shoulder, I saw that he had already moved on, his muscled back receding in the distance until I learned which house was his when he strolled up to the front door and disappeared inside.

And that was how it started. After that day I began to walk by his house each time I visited the old neighborhood, hoping to catch a glimpse of him doing some kind of outdoor chore—mowing the lawn with his T-shirt tucked into the back of his shorts or spraying the grass with a garden hose, sunglasses with white plastic frames perched on his nose. I yearned always for one more glimpse of his face. Those dark eyes and thick brows, cheekbones pressing high toward his temples. Mouth always half-open, thick lips that his tongue would slide over slowly when he was concentrating on something. And over time I became increasingly confident in my invisibility. I believed that this boy really couldn't see me. One day he was outside washing and waxing his father's car, vigorously rubbing a rag in circles over and over again across the maroon paint until it had reached a particularly pleasurable shine. I stopped at the end of his driveway, my head dropping to one side while I watched him work. He never even noticed I was there. On each visit to the old neighborhood, I would get closer and closer to his house, almost as if it was somehow luring me in.

I began thinking about him during the week and making plans for how I would next pursue him. When the next Saturday came, I would walk back and forth in front of his house, trying to see through the windows to determine whether anyone was home. And if I couldn't see inside, I would walk along the fence on the side of the house, peering into the backyard through the slats and the overgrown weeds twined at the base of the wooden posts in my attempt to get closer to him. Sometimes he would be lying on a trampoline in the corner of the yard, looking up at the sky. Or maybe his eyes would be closed as he napped lazily in the sun. Sometimes he would lounge in a plastic folding beach chair with his feet on the railing of the deck, smoking a cigarette while flipping through a magazine, probably looking at pictures of girls. He and his father were making small repairs to the house that summer, and one time I watched them for hours while they painted the deck a deeper shade of brown, both of them shirtless, their skin increasingly speckled with dark paint as they worked.

I was walking alongside the fence one day when I heard a girl's voice coming from the backyard, high-pitched laughter followed by a gentle recrimination as I imagined his hands wandering curiously across her body, testing the limits of what she would allow. She squealed as she told him to stop whatever he was doing to her, but I could already tell by the pitch of her voice that she wasn't pushing him away at all. She wanted whatever it was to continue. And I imagined her before I saw her with my own eyes: blond and blue-eyed, a tank top cut low on her chest, jean shorts frayed just below the barely visible curve of her backside. My hands began to shake with a jealous fury, but I still went to the fence and looked into the backyard to see for myself.

I expected her to be someone I didn't know, a high school girl from some other part of town. But when I looked through the fence I saw that it was only B, the girl who lived next door to my father. She was lying beside the beautiful boy on the trampoline, and his hands were beneath her shirt, cupping her breasts even as she teasingly pushed him away. But then she was the one to unbutton his denim shorts. She was the one to massage him gently through his boxers after he slid his shorts to his knees. And she was the one to sit up on her elbows, pull him out of his underwear, and part her lips in a smile as she leaned down into his lap.

I watched the beautiful boy's face while she pleasured him, his neck arching up against the give of the trampoline bed, his hips rising slightly to push himself deeper into her mouth. He moaned gently as she raised her head and then used her hands for a few brief moments before he came. The shock of witnessing his orgasm was like a crack opening up in the earth beneath my feet, everything rumbling around me and bursting open, like what I imagined would happen during an earthquake, all the houses swallowed up by something more powerful than we ever could have known. And I must have also made a sound with my own body—my own surprise at the sight of him so naked in that way—because both of their heads turned suddenly toward me where my face was pressed against the fence.

"What the fuck," he said loudly in my direction. He must have recognized the shape of me through the wide slats of the fence, or maybe he remembered the color of the bright blue T-shirt I'd been wearing that summer, all the times I'd lingered outside his house, thinking no one had noticed me. I realized only then how obvious I'd been, and the shame of it made me want to sink into the ground and be swallowed up whole.

I saw B recognize me, too, the confusion and hurt on her face turning me into the villain in her version of the story of what took place that afternoon. I was the one who had spied on her and had seen her do this very private thing.

She must have known by then that I'd been avoiding her ever since the afternoon in her basement, and she must have wondered what had scared me off when other boys had clearly wanted her badly enough to beg. Maybe she had spent time in pain afterward but then had become angry at me for rejecting her, finally dismissing me in favor of the older boy down the street who was now sitting up beside her on the trampoline, his body filling with what I recognized as the potential for violence. He hastily pulled up his shorts, buttoning the fly as he leapt down from the trampoline and shouted at me to go away, bolting toward me across the yard.

Now he must have been remembering all the times I'd followed him on those other long weekend afternoons, always watching from my various vantage points where I thought he couldn't see me. He said he would kill me if he could get his hands on me. He threw words at me like bullets, and the one that hung over me as I ran away back down the street was *faggot, faggot, faggot.*

～

I spoke to B only one more time after that. She was waiting on her front porch when my mother dropped off us off the following Saturday, my brother racing off to join a group of kids jumping rope a few houses down while I fumbled with my cooler, pretending not to have seen her there. And even though I pointedly did not look her way, she called out my name and walked over to where I stood awkwardly in the driveway after closing the door to my father's car.

"I'm sorry about what happened," she began, her voice full of a pity that sparked a rage deep in my chest. "I'm sorry about what he said to you."

But I didn't want anyone to feel sorry for me, least of all this girl who now had everything I wanted. And I said unforgivable words to her to make her leave me alone. I made sure she would forever stop trying to be a friend to me, turning my face away from her when I saw the tears spring to her eyes. I told her she was a whore. I said that I couldn't even look at her. I couldn't believe what she had done. I couldn't believe she would do such a horrible, disgusting thing in the clear light of day when anyone at all could walk by and see.

6

MY MOTHER ALWAYS PICKED US UP AT DUSK outside our father's house and drove us back home without ever knowing we hadn't actually gone inside to see him. My fist would be wrapped tightly around the handle of my cooler as we waited at the end of the driveway, my brother perking up excitedly when we saw her car approaching down the street. I didn't tell her about the dangers I'd flirted with by walking alone through the streets, trespassing as though no one could see I was even there. I didn't tell her about the boys I'd watched. And I wouldn't ever have told her what I had been called by the boy I thought I loved, the word slicing through me like a knife.

My brother must have understood things differently at the time. He must not have realized that we were supposed to be visiting our father during the days we spent in the old neighborhood. But I knew he'd become scared of the house, just as I had. The smells, the stains on the floor, the sight of our father unconscious on the couch. I'd probably made up a story to explain why we weren't supposed to tell our father we were there. By that time, I'd come to think of our father's house as haunted, like the boarded up and abandoned Myers house in Haddonfield that Michael inhabits while he waits for darkness to fall on Halloween night after his dramatic escape from the asylum, counting down the minutes until he could emerge onto the streets. I knew I couldn't make myself go inside the house again.

The last time I ever went trick-or-treating was that fall, a couple months after turning twelve, my brother nine years old as he walked beside me from house to house in my father's neighborhood. "There will be better candy there," our mother had said to us as she ushered us out the door toward the car. She was probably remembering the year before, all the townhouses in our new neighborhood with the porch lights turned off, only a few other children wandering the otherwise empty streets as my brother and I walked around at dusk wearing our matching cowboy outfits, the fake leather boots we never wore again. Now she had agreed to cover the beginning of a shift at the bar for a friend who was out sick, and would pick us up in a few hours when another girl could fill in.

"Your father can walk you around," she said in the car on the short drive to his house after I had protested vehemently, not wanting to go back there at all. "Just go inside and let him know you're there. Think of all the candy you'll come home with later."

My mother dropped us off in early evening, as the sun was beginning to set. Ever since I'd seen B and the neighborhood boy on the trampoline three months ago, I'd avoided them at all costs during the Saturday visits to my father's house, hiding in the yard where I knew I wouldn't be seen and reading a book in the shade while my brother played in the street with other kids until our mother arrived to take us home. One day I saw B walking ahead of me on the sidewalk toward her house, and I ran into the backyard of a neighbor I'd never met to hide from her. He yelled at me from the patio where he was sitting with a bottle of beer and a cigar, threatening to call the police if I trespassed again.

Now a chill was creeping into the air on Halloween night as my brother and I stepped out onto the driveway at the old house and closed our mother's car door behind us. "Have fun," she said, already pulling away in a hurry.

Earlier I'd put on my costume in front of the bathroom mirror and then sat at my mother's vanity table to apply the vampire makeup, squeezing it from a thin tube my mother had bought in the seasonal section of the grocery store. White paste for my face, my mouth red with fake blood carefully applied from a tube of lipstick. The plastic fangs dug uncomfortably into my cheeks when I put them on, but I liked the transformation of little boy to monster. My mother even painted a trickle of blood from my lips down to my chin, as if I'd just finished feeding on my latest victim.

My brother was wearing a superhero costume that year, some amalgamation of different popular characters composed of whatever articles of clothing we could find at the secondhand store when my mother remembered at the last minute that we hadn't yet bought new costumes: red cape, green face mask, tight bodysuit emblazoned with fake, exaggerated muscles rippling across his chest and abdomen. I told him he looked like a professional wrestler, not a superhero. I told him he looked like a clown. Then he threw the mask on the floor, and my mother had to console him while he sobbed into her shoulder.

"You're his big brother," she said through her teeth, as if I'd forgotten.

We stood together on the sidewalk outside our father's house, watching the taillights of our mother's car disappear around the corner. My brother looked up at me, holding his empty pillowcase. Other children streamed past us in costumes much more elaborate than ours—more expensive, I knew. Suddenly I was embarrassed about the paint on my face, the stupid red lipstick I'd carefully applied from the drawer of my mother's vanity table. Beads of sweat formed on my brow, and I dabbed them away with my gloved hand.

"Let's go," I said, and we walked briskly past our father's house, avoiding looking in through the windows to see if I might spot him inside sipping one of his beers. But it was all dark anyway, and I saw that not even the porch light was on as we walked toward the next house on the block.

I didn't dare even a glance in the direction of B's house. I also steered us clear of the beautiful boy's house at the end of the block when we'd made it that far down the street, even as part of me was desperate to ring the bell to see what would happen. Maybe he would be holding a plastic pumpkin full of cheap candy ready to drop some into my bag before he recognized me through the makeup and the fake blood. Maybe he'd even be in costume. As we passed his house, I let myself imagine what he'd be—a vampire like me, or perhaps some kind of professional athlete, the uniform tight against his chest, someone else's name in capital letters across the back of a jersey. But I couldn't let my brother see the other boy's reaction to my sudden presence. I couldn't let my brother hear what he would call me if he recognized me—if he saw through my silly costume to what I really was underneath.

"You're walking too fast," my brother said from somewhere behind me on the sidewalk, and I realized I'd been hurriedly steering us to the next block over, where we were less likely to see anyone we knew. I looked back and saw my brother fumbling in the grass for something he had dropped. His hand came up holding a small wrapped candy bar with a shiny label, a look of accomplishment on his face. Before moving on, he peeled it open and tossed it quickly into his mouth, discarding the empty wrapper inside his pillowcase.

"More," he said, chocolate showing in his teeth as he bared them with his mouth open wide. "More!"

I laughed and grabbed his arm, pulling him toward the houses down the next block with porch lights on, fake cobwebs clinging to some of the tree branches along the sidewalk and the distant sound of spooky music guiding us deeper into the night.

Some of the people who opened the doors after we knocked were wearing cartoonish costumes, colorful clown outfits and gorilla suits, characters I recognized vaguely from comic books, superheroes like my brother, then an older man with a long white beard wearing a Batman outfit that hung loosely off his small frame. A woman in her pajamas made us tell her a joke before she dropped individually wrapped candy bars into our pillowcases, and a grandmother gave out candied apples jabbed straight through with sticks that left a syrupy glue on my fingers after I flung mine into the grass after she closed the door. But I jumped back in surprise when the front door of a house just like my father's swung open when I knocked, revealing a dark room full of mannequins made up like corpses and a little girl at the far end of the living room in a pink dress and an exaggerated smile painted onto her face. She was holding a plastic bag full of candy. "Trick or treat," she said, and my brother and I ran screaming back down the porch steps and into the yard.

The sky was completely dark by then. I didn't know what time it was, but I knew we should be heading back to our father's driveway soon, before our mother arrived to pick us up. I couldn't risk her knocking on his door and finding out we'd never told him we were there.

"How much do you have?" I said, gesturing at my brother's pillow-case. He glanced inside and seemed disappointed when he looked back up at me. "Okay," I said, my own bag only half full. "Let's hit a few more houses."

We moved farther down the street, and I realized I didn't know where we were anymore. We'd turned onto the block parallel to my father's, and then we'd run from the house with the mannequins, cutting through a few other yards toward a house with a long line of children, probably one that was giving out something good. Now the houses all looked the same, but I knew we'd never been on that street before. I didn't think I'd even gone that far during my long walks through the neighborhood, my eyes secretly cataloging the details, aware that I was hunting for something I couldn't name.

"A haunted house," said my brother, and it was almost a question coming out of his mouth, as if he couldn't believe his eyes. But then I saw the house up ahead where loud, eerie music was drifting out through an open garage door. A masked Grim Reaper was posted before a curtained doorway leading inside, the furls of his black robe cascading out from hidden feet like the skirt of a Christmas tree waiting to be covered with wrapped gifts. The metal blade of the scythe he held looked real and dangerous. My brother shrank against me, hiding behind my vampire cape, but he didn't object as we approached the house together. And then a gruff voice from behind the Grim Reaper mask said, "Enter if you dare," followed by a laugh made more sinister by the fact that I couldn't see the mouth that had spoken the words.

I didn't force my brother to go inside with me. I wasn't dragging him in against his will as I slipped excitedly into the dark, imagining the Grim Reaper smiling behind his mask as he pulled the curtain aside for me. I didn't tell my brother that he had to see for himself what awaited us in the haunted house. None of it was my fault. And once we were both in the garage, the curtain falling shut behind us as the music grew louder and more ominous by the second—a promise that something impossibly sinister lurked in those deep shadows—I forgot that my brother had even been there with me at all.

My eyes slowly adjusted to the darkness, a flickering bulb on the wall of the garage guiding my way as I held my hands out before me, my fingertips brushing past more curtains hanging from the ceiling in what already seemed like a maze. I saw a few other costumed figures up ahead of me, the path through the bedsheets strung up on the rafters leading us toward a short staircase into what must have been the kitchen of the house, but which had been transformed entirely into a facsimile of a crime scene, a room in which something terrible had happened. Fake blood was smeared on the walls, dripping down the sides of countertops and splashed haphazardly across the kitchen table, the artificial redness visible only by candlelight as I followed the sound of music pulsing from deeper in the house. There was a chalk outline of a body on the tiled floor, limbs splayed out at impossible angles, a deep dark stain at the center. Bloody footprints led farther into the darkness ahead.

I had no choice. I had to see what was waiting for me inside. A scream erupted from somewhere behind me—or maybe it came from farther into the house, through the living room and the hallway now visible ahead of me lined with cheap candelabras and plastic bats dangling from the ceiling, their wings swaying lightly from side to side in the breeze from an open window. The walls of these houses were thin, and sound traveled easily from room to room. The scream could have come from anywhere.

A young woman in a tattered white nightgown suddenly burst into the hallway from an open bedroom door and pushed past the plastic bats, almost knocked down one of the candelabras, and briefly locked eyes with me. Her face was a mask of terror, blood oozing from an open wound on her face, the nightgown drenched in sweat and dirt and more blood, her eyes wide and her mouth hanging open. But no sound was coming out. I couldn't hear anything anymore—the music must have stopped—and she pushed past me, almost slipping on the blood on the kitchen floor as she tore out of the house and into the garage. Then I heard the music again from farther down the hallway, but it was differ-ent now, just a few low piano notes ringing out into the air like a siren singing me home.

I would have walked all the way down the hallway to see what was wait-ing for me there. I would have pushed open a closed door and descended into a dark basement, the wooden steps creaking beneath my feet as I ventured farther and farther into the dark. But as I stepped carefully toward the source of the music, I heard hushed voices on the other side of the wall. A whisper, then a muffled laugh. "My turn," someone said. "You can't have it all for yourself. Come on, pass it down."

I froze in place near the open doorway from which the woman had emerged before—not a woman, I realized then, just a girl, a teenager only two or three years older than me. I'd been thrown off by the look on her face, something she must have practiced beforehand. This was all part of the show. And when I finally mustered the courage to look inside the room from the hallway, peering unseen from the edge of the doorway,

I saw a few figures huddled in the corner of what was just some boy's bedroom, football posters tacked to the walls and trophies lining a shelf above the window. The Halloween decorations hadn't extended into this room, and I felt as if I'd stumbled upon something detached from the reality I'd been in before, like wandering onto a suburban street on the vast red desert of Mars I'd read about in a Ray Bradbury story.

Two boys were passing a bottle between them. I watched one of them pull it to his parted lips and gulp down a few mouthfuls, his throat contracting as he swallowed. The other boy had his arm slung casually across the shoulders of a girl in a cheerleading outfit, perhaps her half-hearted attempt at a costume. He laughed quietly as the boy who was drinking swiped at his cheeks where the booze had slipped from his mouth. And then when I saw his face turn toward the doorway, I knew. Even in the dark, I could tell that he was the boy I'd followed—the boy I'd watched when he didn't know I was there, the boy I'd seen on the trampoline with B. And now here I was in this strange house, which must have been where one of his friends from school lived. I was a vampire lurking in the dark, watching him from the shadows yet again.

I turned around and ran back through the house, knocking aside the cheap decorations and ignoring the music that was now louder and louder in my brain, teasing me with the promise of things even more monstrous and horrible awaiting me. I ran back through the kitchen and into the garage, flailed about when I got caught in one of the sheets, and pushed aside some younger kids whispering excitedly to each other as they moved hesitantly into the haunted house. And then I was outside, still running, the Grim Reaper calling out to me in his normal human voice that eventually faded away into the other sounds of the night— the roar of a truck engine in the distance, shouts of "trick or treat, trick or treat," small children squealing with delight as they amassed piles of candy in their bags.

And then I remembered my brother. I thought he'd been in the house with me when I first stepped inside, but I didn't know when or where I had lost him. I couldn't even remember when I'd last seen him.

I turned back and walked up the driveway to the garage. "I lost my brother," I said to the Grim Reaper, my voice quivering and my hands shaking as I looked up into the black eyes of his oversized skull mask. "Have you seen him? He's dressed like a superhero."

"That's all you've got?" came the voice from inside the Grim Reaper costume. He shrugged somewhere inside his dark robe. "Lots of super-heroes tonight."

He now had the voice of a teenage boy who was probably friends with the other boys I'd seen inside the house. Maybe the girl with the fake wound on her face had been his girlfriend or his sister, someone in on the act. Everything was blurring together in my head. I suddenly wanted everyone out of their costumes, desperately wanted everyone to show their true face. Only then would I be able to find my brother.

The Grim Reaper shrugged again, raising his scythe into the air. "It's Halloween night," he explained.

I called out my brother's name as loudly as I could. I screamed it into the garage of the haunted house, cupping my hands around my mouth. I staggered down the driveway to the sidewalk, looking frantically down the street in both directions for some kind of clue to where he'd gone. He must have been afraid to wander any farther into the haunted house. Maybe he'd grappled for my hands in the dark as I left him behind, too scared to even cry out in the sudden dark for fear of what might have been lurking on the other side of the sheets hanging from the ceiling. Maybe he'd thought something would come bursting out of the shadows and pull him away forever. But I knew he wasn't inside anymore. He wouldn't have stayed there without me. He probably hadn't even seen the bloody kitchen—or maybe that was what he had run away from, imagining that it had been real and that we were in danger if we went any farther.

Hoping for a glimpse of his superhero costume, I scanned children his size at the front doors of houses and on the sidewalks hauling bags of candy down the block. Everything had seemed so bright before, so full of color and light. But now it was all shadows, all those dark and secret places where my brother might have been hiding.

Or worse. Doors through which he might've been taken, snatched up and never seen again.

I didn't even know where I'd left my pillowcase full of candy. Maybe it was somewhere inside the house. I could have dropped it in the hall-way when I ran away after seeing the boy from down the street, this boy with another girl now who wasn't B, this boy who I imagined had some-how lured me into the haunted house without me even knowing he was there. But I didn't care about my lost candy. I had to find my brother. My mother had told me to keep him safe.

I called his name again as I moved down the street, retracing the steps we'd taken toward the haunted house. There was the house where we'd waited on the front porch for a few beats too long after ringing the bell before an old woman with a cane appeared in the doorway with a bowl of jelly beans and a measuring cup for us to scoop out a portion for ourselves. There was the house where I looked into the dark living room and, while the teenage girl rummaged in the bag of miniature chocolate bars for the kind my brother had requested, locked eyes with a boy waiting on the couch for her to come back to join him, a monster movie paused on the screen against the opposite wall. And there was the house where my brother had almost burst into tears when a man in a zombie costume had shambled out of the bushes while we waited at the door, his makeup smeared from sweat.

"Brains," he had drawled, blood and guts spewing from his chest. "Brains, brains, brains."

Up ahead on the sidewalk a little boy was standing alone with his back to me, his superhero cape dangling from one shoulder, the strap on the other side having come loose. I ran up behind him and said my brother's name as I tugged on his shoulder, but when he turned around, with an annoyed expression behind the lightning bolt painted across his face, I saw that he wasn't my brother at all.

"Sorry," I managed to say as he was ambushed by his similarly costumed friends, a little gang of superheroes. He glanced back at me as they rushed off together, almost as if he was worried I'd follow them down the sidewalk all the way home.

And then I was on my father's block again. I'd found no sign of my brother. I'd lost him somewhere in the crowd. Maybe he'd seen another boy my age dressed like a vampire and followed him out of the haunted house, walking a few houses down the block before he realized his mistake. After all, I'd been hurrying all night, leaving him scrambling behind. He could have thought I'd gone on ahead without him and had rushed to each house hoping to catch me before I moved on.

I knew even then that I was not always kind to him—was not often kind. Sometimes I'd see him watching me, studying me like some kind of detective. I didn't like to think about what he might have been seeing when he looked at me, so I would scream and scream at him to stop staring, to mind his own business, wishing he would just worry about his own frail and weak body, his own struggle to navigate the edges of the childhood we'd found ourselves in. Maybe he was already used to being abandoned and left behind by me, and this night was no different from all the others.

Or maybe he'd been lured into the shadows by someone in a friendly costume with the promise of candy who would then shed the mask as soon as he led my brother too far from the street to be heard if he cried out. I'd read so many stories like that. I'd thought about it happening to me, too, wondering whether I'd run away or simply accept my fate, following this stranger into the dark.

Maybe T had also gone trick-or-treating that night, costumed and giggling with her friends as they wandered around pretending to be zombie cheerleaders or a band of punk rockers who only went outside in the dark. She would not be alive to see another Halloween.

I finally told myself that my brother had just gotten lost. Maybe he was confused and had wandered farther into the neighborhood, the houses all looking the same at night, and he would wander and wander long after we were supposed to be picked up to go home. I'd have to tell my mother I'd lost him. I'd have to ride in the passenger seat as we drove slowly around the neighborhood, my mother sobbing as we called my brother's name over and over again out the open windows even though all the lights had long ago gone dark. But then suddenly, through the throngs of costumed children and impatient parents waiting on the sidewalk with strollers and on dark lawns covered in candy wrappers, I saw my mother and my brother up ahead at the end of my father's driveway. The little superhero was heaving with sobs, his face against her chest while she held him close.

She finally saw me when I stepped into the glow of the streetlight, and soon she was wiping away the tears now streaming down my own cheeks. My brother wouldn't even look at me as he dried his eyes with my mother's shirt.

"You left him," said my mother.

"I lost him."

My brother said, "You were swallowed up by the haunted house."

"Where was your father?" said my mother.

"Everybody was a vampire," said my brother. "But none of them were you."

"Why aren't you with your father?" said my mother again.

I finally blurted out, "He doesn't know we're here. He never knows we're here."

Then I was crying again as my mother pulled me close and the three of us cried together, in the front yard where we'd once chased each other through the sprinkler on hot summer days, the same yard where we'd planted the tree after the tornado, just off the front porch in front of my bedroom window, its branches already bare that late in the season.

We waited in our mother's car while she went to the door and knocked, knocked again, waiting for my father to appear. The windows of the house were all dark, but he was holding a bag of candy when he opened the door. He was expecting to see a group of children in costumes, but instead he saw only my mother, the shoulders of her sweatshirt over her bartending outfit still wet with our tears. My father took a step back, steadying himself against the doorframe at the entrance to his house. Then he looked out at the car and caught my eye through the window, confusion exploding across his face.

"I didn't know," I imagined him saying. I couldn't hear anything from inside the car. "They didn't come to the door. I never knew you had dropped them off. How was I supposed to know?"

"He lost his brother," I imagined my mother saying, but in a way that blamed my father for what happened instead of me, even though I was the only one at fault. I saw her point her index finger at his chest as if it would stab right through him, saw my father shake his head and toss the candy aside and press his hands together as if to ask for forgiveness. Then I saw him glance my way again as my mother stalked down the walkway toward the car, the keys in her fist glinting in the light as she fumbled with the door and finally launched herself into the driver's seat.

I looked through the rear window of the car as we pulled away for what would be the last time. The trick-or-treaters were mostly back home inside their own houses with their bags of candy by then, but a few costumed figures still roamed the shadows. I pretended to be Michael Myers hunting for my next victim, looking for the most vulnerable person to attack. But there was just my father. He had stepped out onto the porch and was standing next to the plastic chair where he would often sit with a beer and his pack of cigarettes when we all still lived there together, those long afternoons when he had watched my brother and me playing in the yard, warning us not to get too close to the road. Now he was holding the bag of candy again in case any children saw that he was home and came wandering up to the house, opening their bags for whatever he had to offer them.

I pressed my hand to the window, but my father only stood there unmoving in the deepening darkness, smaller and smaller in the distance until I couldn't tell him apart from any of the ghosts still roaming the mostly empty streets.

7

Dr. Loomis trails Michael all the way back to Haddonfield after his escape from the asylum on the hunch that his patient would instinctively return home once he'd broken free. We see Loomis pulled over at a roadside phone booth, frantically calling the local authorities to warn them about what's coming their way. Loomis hangs up only to discover Michael's discarded hospital uniform in an abandoned truck on a dirt road just past the phone booth. And as he rushes back to his car with renewed urgency, the camera pans to reveal the body of a murdered auto repairman from whom Michael has recently acquired his black coveralls.

Loomis later arrives in town and approaches the sheriff on the street, and the two men drive to the Myers house to search for evidence that Michael has indeed come home. The house looks abandoned and in disrepair, almost as if it's been forgotten over the passage of time, its shabby white exterior framed against a near total darkness. "Every kid in Haddonfield believes this place is haunted," says the sheriff as they approach the front door. And when he and Loomis enter the house, the paint that had once seemed so fresh back when Michael was a child is now peeling off the walls in strips, the windows boarded up, the staircase railing chipped and discolored. The empty rooms have been stripped of furniture, and the whole house seems to sag with the weight of what had happened here.

"I met this six-year-old child with this blank, pale, emotionless face," Loomis says as he tries to explain the root of his fears. "And the blackest eyes. The devil's eyes. I spent eight years trying to reach him, and then another seven trying to keep him locked up, because I realized that what was living behind that boy's eyes was pure and simply *evil*."

Loomis agrees to keep watch at the house while the sheriff goes off to investigate the darkening streets of Haddonfield for any sign of Michael, and he scares off a few children who show up early on Halloween night, titillated by the old and abandoned house's reputation and approaching the front porch with a giddy apprehension. The sheriff reappears and says he's found no evidence that Michael has returned. But Loomis remains unconvinced.

"I watched him for fifteen years," he says, his words heavy with all that he has seen. "Sitting in a room, staring at a wall. Not seeing the wall, looking past the wall. Looking at *this night*, inhumanly patient, waiting for some secret, silent alarm to trigger him off." The empty Myers house looms behind him as he speaks, a low-angle shot making the house appear to be almost larger than life, its lingering evils seeping out beyond the otherwise benign plot of land on which it rests. "Death has come to your little town," he concludes.

A harbinger of doom. A promise of death.

When I first heard these words in my father's living room as darkness fell on the street outside the window, I already had a sense that my presence in my own Haddonfield was that of a potential scourge that would infect all those around me. I didn't belong on those quiet streets where children were playing innocently on the sidewalks. I was a monster in the shadows, a danger to warn other kids against. When Loomis and the sheriff looked for Michael in the empty house, it felt as if they were looking for me instead, trying to root me out and expose me for what I was. I was peering into all those dark corners at the Myers house to see where he might hide, and wondering if maybe I could join him there.

I'd always known intuitively that I had to keep myself hidden away, but not inside my father's house, which now resembled the Myers house in its neglect and squalor, the once-welcoming front door having become a threshold that could never again be crossed. My brother and I weren't allowed to see our father unsupervised after the Halloween night when my mother discovered the truth about our visits, and I didn't think much about the old house anymore after that. I didn't miss it. It was a relief to not be made to return there and face the memories trapped inside. The house we'd once all shared together was now haunted and needed to be boarded up, its demons and ghosts trapped inside forever, even with my father still there alone in the dark behind the locked front door.

~

I didn't know yet that my father was sick, and had probably been sick for a while. None of us could have known. After all, we hadn't actually seen him in months until that last Halloween night outside his house. My mother called me down to the kitchen table one afternoon early that winter while I was playing a video game with my brother upstairs. We were racing each other to the finish in a track made up like a haunted house, little ghosts popping out from the side as diversions to knock us to the depths below as we drove madcap through the narrow pathways. My mother yelled my name from the kitchen just as I was about to navigate the final turn toward the finish line.

"I didn't want to tell you in front of your brother," she said when we heard the game resume upstairs as my brother continued playing without me, the familiar notes of its background music ringing through the house. I sat there numb at the kitchen table, trying to absorb the news she'd just shared with me and imagining the ghosts in the video game— what happened after we left our bodies behind forever.

I learned not to say the word in front of my brother, but it quickly became the only thing I could think about, the seeds of death now visible all around me. How oblivious I'd been not to have noticed it before. Now I'd see cancer in every common cold or flu I suffered, the onset of an incurable disease, something I already understood by then from harrowing news reports to be inevitable for people like me. I'd see cancer in the old people hunched over their shopping carts at the supermarket, their gray skin dotted with purple blotches. I'd see cancer even in the other kids at school, inspecting their skin from afar for signs of blight, even as I knew that sickness usually started in the places we couldn't see, taking root deep inside our bodies before making itself known.

I'd see cancer in the people in the long hallway as I passed them in the dream, the skin of their faces peeled back to reveal the rot of their insides, veins and organs all crawling with worms.

Now after the diagnosis we had to visit our father in the hospital instead of at the old house. We drove one night for almost an hour on the highway as the sky grew dark, lights blinking on in other towns in the distance as happy families settled in for the evening, and we crossed the river into St. Louis as the black water churned below us. My mother had always been afraid of bridges, once telling me that she always worried she would get to the center and then the bridge would suddenly collapse beneath her, sending her hurtling into the icy cold waters below. She said that if she was caught in traffic on the bridge on her way home from work, she would cry the whole time, tears rolling silently down her cheeks. She laughed when she told me this, making herself seem silly. But I took bridges seriously after that.

"Hold your breath," I whispered to my brother that night on our way to see our father at the hospital, and we sucked the air into our lungs and didn't exhale until we were safely over to the other side, back on solid ground.

I hadn't been inside a hospital since my brother had suffered a bout of pneumonia a few years before. The lights in the hallways were all too bright, and the elevator smelled as if it had been scrubbed clean with a dangerous chemical. After stepping into a hallway full of busy nurses running back and forth with clipboards, my mother steered us to a seating area while she went to the nurses' station to ask for directions to our father's room. Two old women were sitting across from us, one of them knitting a scarf and the other trembling with her hand at her mouth and her eyes closed tight as she whispered a prayer. I thought of all my own prayers that had gone unanswered.

"This way," said my mother finally, and we scrambled toward her and walked a few doors past the reception desk to the room where my father was waiting for us. I remember it being small and cramped and dimly lit, any free space occupied by the various machines to which my father's body was attached. Long beeps emitted rhythmically from the multicolored screens next to his bed, broadcasting information in a coded language that I didn't know how to decipher.

We hadn't seen him since that Halloween night a couple months before, and my mother had prepared us in the hospital parking lot before we went inside.

"He won't look the same," she said, turning around to face us from the driver's seat. She looked exhausted. I noticed the first wrinkles beginning to form around her eyes and the corners of her lips as she sucked down the last of the cigarettes she'd been smoking out the open window during the entire drive to the hospital, the smell now clinging to my T-shirt as I walked into my father's hospital room. I was holding a book about vampires that I planned to show him because he had never gotten to see my Halloween costume up close. The cover of the book was a black-and-white photograph of a movie star in a dark suit with fangs protruding from his open mouth. He had his arms raised at his sides, a cape unfurling behind him like the wings of a bat.

Many years later, my mother would tell me about how my father had been made to sober up just to be treated at the hospital. She said he'd shaken violently and uncontrollably, cursing and thrashing and needing to be held down by several nurses before the delirium had passed. I don't know why she was the one who had to be there for him, but maybe he'd asked for her. Maybe she was the only one he trusted to see him that way. She told me how his eyes were desperate and angry and frightened and devastated all at the same time, as if he were watching himself from outside his body, knowing how pitiful he looked, how tragic and lost.

"I'd rather be dead," he'd finally managed to say. "Anything but this."

And she just squeezed his hand while he jerked from side to side as though he was suffering a seizure, something inside of him clawing its way out. But when I saw him in the hospital for the first time, he looked only saggy and deflated, like whatever had been keeping his body in its human shape was gone and this was what had been left behind in its place.

My mother had gone into the room first to make sure he was ready to see us, and I almost didn't recognize him until he smiled at me where I was frozen in the doorway. The room was dark and full of shadows at the edges, but it was as if a spotlight had been set up right above my father's bed, so white that it glowed. The lights on the machines pumping liquids into his body through translucent tubes were blinking like the lights of a spaceship, impossible to comprehend because it had come from so far away.

My brother began to cry immediately.

"I'll take him outside," said my mother, my brother burying his face in her chest as she guided him back out the door. And then I was alone with my father. We hadn't spoken in months.

"You look good," he said. His voice had a crackle in it that needed to be ironed out. "You're so much bigger than before."

"I grew three inches in the fall," I said.

"You're taller than I am now," he said proudly, and I blushed. Then he added, "I wish you'd come inside the house before. She told me she's been dropping you off."

"I'm sorry," I mumbled. I couldn't look at him.

"I'll make it better," he said. "The house. I'll fix it up. For next time."

We listened to the machine beeping next to him, the jagged lines on the screen drawing a picture of his heartbeat. I understood that something was attacking my father from the inside. I wanted to know if he could feel it as I did—if he'd known it was there the whole time but had been powerless against it, his body taken over by something he couldn't control.

"Does it hurt?" I asked, staring at the tubes pumping liquids into his veins through the needle taped to the wrist of his good arm, the other curled limply at his side as always. Maybe I could be saved that way too.

"I don't feel anything at all," he said. "Most of the time it's like I'm somewhere else. Somewhere far away."

My father's eyes went blurry, as if he was having trouble focusing on me there in the room with him. I squirmed in the metal chair and looked down at the floor.

"I've been having these dreams," he continued in a faraway voice. My mother had warned me about the drugs for the pain, how he might not act like himself. "I was afraid the first time it happened. I thought I'd died, like the dream was where I'd have to be forever."

He laughed weakly, later describing his embarrassment at having had to be comforted by a nurse like a child. "And the dream," he said. He shook his head from side to side, as if to break a spell that had been cast on him. "I can't explain it, but it's like I'm moving forward in the dark—"

My father couldn't have known about the long hallway. I had never told anyone about the dream. But now it was as if we were walking together past all those doomed people at the edges of the wall in the dark—the people whose eyes I couldn't stop seeing, even when I was fully awake. The man was waiting for us at the end of the hallway, and we had to keep moving forward no matter what happened. Maybe my father had been beside me the whole time on all those other nights, and I just hadn't looked to see.

"Look who's ready to see his dad," said my mother from behind me in the doorway. My brother had wiped the tears from his eyes, and now I watched him take a tentative step into the room. My father patted the white sheet beside him on the bed, and my brother and I sat awkwardly on the plastic-covered mattress, careful not to disturb any of the medical equipment. I finally showed him the book about vampires, my brother turning the pages with me. We looked through the old movie stills together, marveling at how believably the otherwise perfectly ordinary male actor had been transformed so completely into a monster.

"Look at that one," I said. The vampire was standing on the stone balcony of a castle, his head thrown back and his mouth open wide.

"What big teeth you have," said my father, noticing the sharp fangs in the vampire's mouth already dripping with the blood of a recent victim.

"The better to eat you with, my dear," I said, doing my best wolf voice.

Eventually a nurse poked her head into the room to let us know that visiting hours were over. We awkwardly hugged our father goodbye, avoiding the tubes and the machines, the wires tangled up together on the floor next to his bed. And then we were gone.

~

My father was discharged after a long stay in the hospital. He'd undergone an experimental treatment and his cancer was now in remission, but I was still afraid of him when I saw him for the first time after the hospital at my grandparents' house, remembering all the tubes he had been attached to and how he had seemed almost more machine than human. When he swept me up in a hug after he saw me hanging back at the front door, I looked for signs of scars on his wrist where the needles had been inserted, evidence of the sickness that had taken over his body. But it was as if none of it had ever happened at all. He was my father again.

"Was he drinking at dinner?" my mother asked after she picked us up and began the drive back home, meeting my eyes in the rearview mirror as she pulled onto the main road from the gravel driveway of my grandparents' house.

I nodded slowly, remembering that he'd asked me to get him a cold one to replace the empty he was holding when we were outside by the fire pit, then another when he stood up unsteadily to drive home. My mother's lips disappeared in a frown as she reached for a pack of cigarettes in the

80

glove compartment, cupped her hands around a lighter to keep the flame from burning out.

Only a month or so after that day, my mother sat me down and told me that my father had finally lost the old house. He'd have to live somewhere else. At first I thought of the tornado, imagining that something had stormed through and lifted the house right up into the air, leaving my father alone in the empty yard, looking bewilderedly up at the sky. "He couldn't keep up with the payments anymore," said my mother, trying to explain to me what had happened. And then it all made sense. She was chopping potatoes at the kitchen counter, then putting water in a pot to boil. "You probably won't see him for a while."

We had recently moved to a larger, newly built house in a subdivision just off the highway a few exits west of where we'd lived before in the townhouse, a planned community with several almost-identical houses surrounding a small pond with a fountain in the center that came on automatically every morning. My brother and I had been fighting all the time in our shared bedroom in the townhouse, sometimes violently. One time we'd been playing cards on the top bunk and I'd shoved him hard when I thought I'd caught him cheating. Shocked by the strength of my hands against his chest, he caught my eye as fear blazed across his face and he tumbled backward and landed hard on the floor below, the carpet barely breaking his fall. He screamed and howled in pain, holding an injured arm close to his chest until my mother came running up the stairs to see what I had done.

"We can't keep on like this," she said to me, her face slack and tired, probably remembering all the other times she had been made to protect my brother from me. "You're going to kill each other if you keep sharing this room. Something has to change."

My mother gave me a brochure for the new neighborhood that I held onto until we finally moved in, the pages creased from continuous handling. I memorized the contours of the houses pictured and pretended that we were already there, already living in the sunny neighborhood with the pond and the fishing dock at the center, all the houses with a view of the water. The boy living in the model home featured in the brochure was just a few years older than me, wearing a tank top and red shorts as he tossed a basketball into a hoop above his family's garage door, a facsimile of the house that was already being built for us according to our specifications. When I was alone, I would trace the image of him over and over again with my hand, running my fingertips up and down the sides of his body and face.

We no longer lived within walking distance of my father's old house, so I couldn't just stroll down the road or dash through the trees anymore to see what it looked like without my father inside it. But I later asked my mother to drive by the house on the way home from a doctor's appointment, and at first I couldn't even remember which house on the street had been ours, how different everything seemed now, how little remained of what it had been before. My old friends probably still lived there, but we'd lost touch with all of them by then. We didn't go to that school anymore.

I don't know what happened to the copy of *Halloween* that my father had never returned to the video store, whether he took it with him when he moved away, packing it into one of the duffel bags that contained the few items of clothing he owned that weren't stained or ruined, or just left it there forgotten in a drawer to be taken away as trash. I don't know if he ever watched it on those long nights alone after we were gone, or maybe even on those nights when we were supposed to be visiting him but never made our presence known. All I saw when we drove past the house that final time was the memory of my father standing on the front porch and watching us drive away on Halloween night, wiping the sleep from his eyes and trying to make sense of what had happened. Trying to understand why we'd never gone inside to let him know we were there.

I didn't see my father for a while after he lost the house. We didn't hear anything about where he was living, what he was doing, whether he was having any luck finding work. Whether he was still healthy or whether the cancer had come back. And then one day in early spring he called my mother and asked if he could see us on a Saturday afternoon in the park. He would drive out to our town from wherever it was that he was staying. And I didn't know it yet, but this was when he wanted to talk to me about girls.

I couldn't have known that it would be the last time I'd ever see him. I was still thinking about the hospital, remembering the version of my father that I'd seen there. But then as my mother angled the car into a parking spot beneath the outstretched branches of a tree, I saw him already sitting on the bench at the picnic table. He smiled when he caught my eye. "Michael Myers," he said affectionately when I was close enough to hear his voice.

It was a beautiful day. T was still alive then. It wouldn't be dark for hours. My father pretended to be holding a knife.

~

We hadn't lived in the new house for even a full year when T was murdered. The days were getting longer, buds sprouting on the trees up at the top of the small hill behind the house where wildflowers grew in the brush. I'll always remember closing the door of my own bedroom for the first time after the moving trucks pulled away and realizing that I finally had a space all to myself—a door I could lock to keep everyone out. That small room no bigger than a twin bed and a small desk would become a whole world to me in the years that followed, a container for my secret self. Only there would he ever see the light of day.

I'd chosen that room because of the window seat facing the pond, a carpeted ledge where I'd sit cross-legged for hours, reading or watching the neighborhood outside as day turned to night—young couples pushing strollers down the sidewalk, teenagers holding hands who probably thought no one could see. I'd noticed a boy down the street and imagined him to be the one whose picture I'd traced with my fingertips in those months while we'd waited for the new house to be finished, how alike they seemed to me. One Friday afternoon after school as I rode my bike slowly past his house, secretly hoping to get another glimpse of him, he was outside and introduced himself to me. He had never talked to me on the bus rides home from school, but now he was asking for my name. He had shaggy hair that he ran his fingers through whenever he could, dimples that flared up when he smiled, and narrow cheeks I'd learn later would flush bright red when he was angry.

"You're new here," he said after waving at me from his front yard where he was tinkering with the gears of an old bicycle. I nodded to him as I rolled to a stop at the base of his driveway. "My sister says you're good at video games." She was in my class at school, and he would start high school after the upcoming summer break.

"I guess," I answered. Maybe she'd overheard me in the cafeteria bragging about being the first in my class to reach the final boss battle of a newly released RPG. She could have even been making fun of me when she mentioned to her brother that there was this fragile boy living in the new house down the street who spent all his time alone. But I didn't care, because then he was inviting me over to hang out with him later that night. A friend had bailed on him in favor of a girl who'd agreed last minute to join him at the movies.

"You can show me some of your moves," he said.

My brother had plans to stay overnight with a new friend down the block, and I would otherwise have been alone with my thoughts on another long night locked up in my bedroom while my mother worked late at the computer downstairs. I immediately agreed to come over later, and back at home I stood in front of my closet for what seemed like hours trying to figure out how best to seem like all the other boys so that he wouldn't immediately send me away. Then I began to fear that he was playing a joke on me and that he'd laugh and laugh when I arrived at the house, mocking me for how I eager I was for his company. How I'd actually believed he wanted me to be his friend. But later I made myself walk back up the street at dusk, my stomach in knots until he answered my hesitant knock on the door and flashed his easy smile.

He held the door open for me and our chests almost touched in the small foyer as I slipped past him, all too aware of the feeling of his hot breath on my neck as I angled my head away from his. I realized quickly that the house had the same layout as ours, but in perfect reverse. The living room opened to the right instead of the left as I stepped inside. The kitchen was on the opposite side, the view from the window above the sink looking down the hill toward my own house rather than up toward the highway as ours did. And I was unnerved to imagine the second floor, just up the staircase around the corner to my right. My brother's bedroom would be on the wrong side of the hallway, everything backward and impossible, as in the Escher print my mother had hung in the bathroom that her boss had given us as a housewarming gift.

But the other boy didn't invite me to explore the house further. Instead, he nodded his head in the direction of the open door to the basement, and soon we were downstairs playing the new game on the Nintendo console that my grandparents had given to my brother and me for Christmas. I was showing him the trick to finishing off the last boss in the dungeon—I'd casually told him I'd mastered it when I saw the game paused on the TV after he'd led me downstairs. I also noticed his father's hunting equipment in a far corner, rifles leaning against the wall and camouflage gear folded in neat stacks on a set of metal shelves. Dusty old sports trophies were turned outward above the television screen. I thought of B's basement where we'd spent all those afternoons together before she ruined everything.

"Prove it," he said, handing me the controller.

He kept tucking his hair behind his ears when it came loose as he leaned toward the TV to play, gripping the controller with everything he had and jerking it from side to side as he tried to dodge a fireball, his face wrenched with concentration. He was wearing cotton shorts and a loose blue tank top, his whole bare chest and torso visible through the cutout in the fabric when he slouched forward. I could have stared at him forever, but I forced myself to look at the screen and show him how to finish the fight.

He attempted the battle over and over again after I'd shown him the trick maneuver, our eyes blurry at the edges and discarded cans of Coke crumpled at our feet where we huddled close to each other on an old couch covered in matted fur from a cat I never saw. He finally threw the controller onto the carpet and said, "I give up. I'm never going to figure it out."

Then he scrambled up the stairs, his bare feet padding lightly on the wooden boards, and I pulled the edges of a blanket over my shoulders to fight the chill. I didn't want to be alone.

His scent hung in the air around me as I listened to his footsteps above me in the kitchen. I realized he must have been wearing some kind of body spray, the synthetic smell reminding me of the locker room at school, older boys getting dressed after a shower and rubbing deodorant into their underarms. His sister was out with her friends at the mall and his parents were at a party that some of our new neighbors were throwing down the street, so we had the whole house to ourselves. And when he came back down to the basement, he was carrying a nearly full bottle of brown liquor, a brand I recognized from the shelf in my father's old kitchen below the TV where he'd watched baseball games on weekend afternoons while I was in the other room watching *Halloween*.

"What do you think?" said the older boy. The bottle was now propped between us on the couch, nestled between the two old cushions. The video game was still paused on the screen.

I'd sipped from my father's beer a few times when he told me I could, the two of us sitting on the porch at the old house watching the sky grow dark. I remembered the beer I'd drank alone in my old bedroom years before, the world slipping away behind my closed eyes. And I told this boy I was up for whatever he'd brought downstairs with him. As he took the bottle to his lips, he looked for a moment like his own father, whom I'd seen several times leaning against the house while taking a break from mowing the lawn, wiping his sweaty brow with the hem of an old shirt. Or maybe this boy looked like what his father would be if he had been trimmed down to size—beard shaved, no gray in his hair, muscles softened into more delicate curves up his arms and across his chest.

I saw him swallow twice, his throat contracting as he pulled the liquor down, and he held his hand over his mouth as he passed the bottle to me. "The elixir of the gods," he said finally, making a gag face. Then I took the bottle myself, and I loved the warmth that suddenly sprang up in my chest when I swallowed the first gulp, almost like this boy had brought that warmth into me all by himself—as if it was all because of him that I suddenly felt light-headed and alive, the world settling around me like the calm after a storm.

We passed the bottle back and forth until the booze had lost its sting, the video game still paused on the TV, and I must have dozed off beside him on the couch. I woke up when I felt the other boy's arm slung over me, his fingers moving slowly back and forth across my chest over my thin T-shirt. I leaned more heavily toward him with the instinct of someone who was in no state to question what it was that he desired. I wanted the warmth of his body against mine more than anything else in the world. But then, just as his lips grazed my ear when I nestled closer than I ever would have dared without the fuzziness of the booze, he shoved me away from him with the force of a man bigger than either of us.

I rolled off the couch onto the floor, and I cried out as my head knocked hard against the concrete. A sharp pressure behind my eyes overtook the gentle fuzziness from before, but I went numb after he kicked me in the chest when I tried to stand up to face him. I coughed and struggled to catch my breath even as I tried desperately to think of some way to explain what had happened. A way to make everything right again, to go back to how it had been before. Then he kicked the bottle to its side and sent it rolling across the concrete floor, and I knew I needed to get out. I knew what could happen there. I remembered my father.

I got to my feet and somehow found the staircase from the basement and scrambled up on all fours. Then I turned the wrong way by accident at the top of the stairs, forgetting how everything there was a mirror image of my own house. I was too far from the front door as I plunged through the living room toward what I knew would be another way out, imagining the other boy bolting up the stairs after me as I knocked hard into an end table, pain searing up from my hips even as I kept running and almost slipped on a plastic cat toy, barely righting myself with a palm pressed to the wall and narrowly avoiding taking down a collage of framed family photographs in the process. I left the house through the unlocked sliding door leading onto the patio, breathless and dizzy, the pain from everything that had happened finally dulling even as the memories became hazier, the events of the past few minutes filtered then through the speed at which everything had changed.

I walked the short distance home, six houses down through the dark neighborhood, past the reach of the pale glow from the headlights of cars racing by on the nearby highway. The world was still spinning around me when I fell to my knees and retched onto the grass sloping down to the drainage ditch alongside the road, the vomit coming out thin and sour, bits of bile splashing onto my blue sneakers, creating stains that would never come out.

The night was so quiet that I could already hear the music my mother was playing as I finally turned onto the driveway and went around the house to the unlocked patio door. She'd begun handling the bookkeeping for her boyfriend's construction company, and she would usually spend Friday nights working at the desk in the living room and looking over her shoulder occasionally from the computer at whatever was playing on television. But then I saw her through the window moving slowly through the first floor of the house holding a cigarette and a glass of pink wine, bending her knees in time with the music. I had never seen my mother dance before. And the look on her face when I was close enough to notice reminded me of how she'd looked in the pictures I'd seen in the old album from before she married my father. She was smiling as if she had a secret meant for only her to know, like she'd traveled through

87

time and become someone else—some other version of what she had dreamed for herself.

This was the woman she became when my brother and I weren't there to see her, when she had the whole night alone.

I walked as close to the glass as I dared and then sat down on the cool grass of our small backyard and watched her as the music poured from the radio on the fireplace mantel, the delicate pluck of guitar strings, a man's voice gently serenading her. I knew I couldn't go inside. I couldn't disrupt her moment—the music, the wine, this man's beautiful voice. She would smell the filth clinging to me, would see my dirty clothes and the redness of my eyes. She would know I'd done something wrong. Something unforgivable.

Instead, I just kept watching her. At one point she looked out the window right at where I was sitting, and even as my heart caught in my chest, I knew that the darkness outside was so complete that she could see only her reflection in the glass. She hesitated for a moment and brought her hand to her face, as if to correct something out of place that she had seen there, something wrong that she could fix. Then the song changed, and she closed her eyes, swaying slowly back and forth as the smile returned to her lips.

I waited until she made her way upstairs to bed before I finally went inside.

8

LAURIE STRODE'S BEST FRIEND, Annie, is the first character to be killed on-screen in *Halloween* following Michael's escape from the asylum. Both young women have arrived for babysitting shifts in houses across the street from one another as the cross-cut scene begins, the space between them often depicted through a window at night, barely discernible shapes lurking in the shadows under the blanket of darkness that has descended over Haddonfield.

We already know that Michael is watching because we hear his labored breathing behind his mask as he spies on Annie making popcorn in the kitchen at the Wallace house where she's looking after a little girl named Lindsey. After a flirtatious phone conversation with her boyfriend, Annie calls to ask Laurie to watch Lindsey while she goes to pick him up. Laurie reluctantly agrees as she wipes her hands of the innards of a pumpkin she has been carving with Tommy. Annie soon drops Lindsey off across the street at the Doyle residence, and the two children immediately become mesmerized by a television broadcast of *The Thing from Another World*. Earlier, while Lindsey was watching the same film at her own house with Annie, a group of confused scientists had encircled a flying saucer that had crash-landed on earth. Now the Thing has been found frozen inside the mysterious spacecraft and is slowly coming to life as it thaws, soon to be revealed as a grave danger to all mankind.

Annie heads back across the street and slips into the front seat of a car in the garage, but before she has a chance to insert the key into the ignition, Michael begins choking her from behind. She thrashes about and tries to break free, her eyes alive with terror. And then Michael brings out the knife. Soon afterward, Tommy is hiding behind a curtain across the street, pretending to be the bogeyman to scare Lindsey, who sits rapt on the couch watching the screen as a mysterious spaceship arrives in the distance. Then Tommy turns around slowly to face the window, still concealed by the curtain, and sees Michael carrying Annie's body around the side of the Wallace house and into the front door.

"The bogeyman's outside!" he exclaims. But Michael is already gone when Laurie comes to the window. The house across the street looks as quiet and peaceful as ever.

"Nobody believes me," says Tommy, slinking dejectedly back toward the couch, and the two children resume watching the film while Laurie rolls her eyes up at the ceiling. On the TV screen, the spaceship has descended and is latching onto earthly soil. The sound is something like a train whistling endlessly between the hollow walls of an echo chamber.

Something has arrived.

~

After so many repeat viewings, my favorite parts of *Halloween* became the scenes just before Michael steps out of the shadows to claim his victims. I found comfort in knowing things that the characters themselves would never have suspected, and I was especially thrilled by the moments when I could see from the horrified expressions on their faces that they've just realized what was about to happen to them—and that it was already too late to run.

There was a kind of safety in looking through the eyes of the bogeyman and knowing that I wasn't the one he was after. And I was always so tense with anticipation when I saw Laurie and Annie's friend Lynda pull up to the Wallace house with her boyfriend Bob after dark, beers already in hand, expecting Annie to still be there babysitting Lindsey. The young couple will not live to find out what has happened to their friend, and I watched from Michael's vantage point in the next room as they begin to make out on the couch in what they have discovered is a seemingly empty house. I liked how he didn't even try to conceal himself, just stood there facing them down with all the confidence in the world.

After having sex upstairs, Lynda sends Bob down to the refrigerator for another beer. Michael has been watching them the whole time, his dark shadow drifting into view on the far wall just as Bob reaches climax and slides off Lynda over to the other side of the bed. When she welcomes him into the bedroom again, Lynda slowly reveals her breasts from behind a sheet until her bare chest is fully visible, smiling seductively because she knows what Bob wants.

"See anything you like?" she asks.

She thinks she understands the nature of his desire, and she thinks she knows how to satisfy it. But she doesn't yet know that the man she assumes is Bob is actually Michael Myers in disguise. She doesn't know that he has stabbed Bob to death in the kitchen downstairs after rushing out at him from the shadows, and that what he desires from her now is something entirely different.

I knew when I saw the scene that I should also want to look at Lynda. I understood that what she expected Bob to gawk at was something I was also expected to want. The experience of adolescence as a closeted queer boy is one of constantly attempting to imitate the expression of a desire that you do not feel. I would nod my head when boys at school talked about particular girls, would snicker alongside everyone else when we saw the outline of a substitute teacher's nipples through her blouse or caught a glimpse of the young music teacher's panties when she crossed her legs at the front of the room, something sick always coiling up inside me while I hid behind the louder noises that the other boys would make.

Lynda's mistake is made possible by the fact that Michael as Bob is not only wearing the familiar mask, the cheap plastic that always hides his face. He's also wearing a white sheet that covers his entire body in a performance of the classic Halloween ghost costume, with Bob's glasses resting delicately on his face where his own eyes are obscured by the sheet. The imitation is deliberate and well imagined. He's wearing a mask over a mask. And he seems so cartoonish in this moment, his desire to conceal himself having reached the level of self-parody.

How silly it looks to hide in plain sight.

～

I first heard of conversion therapy on a TV talk show. A young man was asked to confront his mother, who had sent him to a camp years before where he was compelled to pray away whatever had gone wrong inside him. I would pray for the same thing every night at my bedside, knobby knees pressed into the carpet. I would have given anything.

I was going to church on Sundays with my grandmother, and we listened to the sermon and sang the hymns and afterward ate cookies in the basement lounge with the women whom my grandmother volunteered with at the local library—the same library where I'd often hole myself away in a quiet corner with books from the sex education section, flipping through the pages and burning the pictures and drawings into my mind so I could remember them later, the closest thing to pornography I could find. A librarian had once caught me breathlessly flipping through the pages of a book about male puberty, and I'd tossed it aside and scampered away to another aisle, my heart thudding in my chest and my face burning hot with shame. But in the church pew I would fix my gaze on the cross above the altar and beg to be made right. If Laurie's final confrontation with Michael was to signify her deliverance into the dark knowledge of adulthood, I saw adolescence as the time when I would have to face my own bogeyman, and I didn't know yet whether I would survive the encounter.

I had always resented girls like Annie and Lynda. Girls like T. I would try to will myself to find these girls desirable, thinking that if I thought about them hard enough and fantasized about them as earnestly as possible I might somehow trick my body into wanting them. I tried to picture what it would be like to have them in my arms while I touched myself and desperately urged my body to respond—tried to imagine the reveal of bare flesh as my fingertips were invited to roam at will and their own hands eagerly clasped mine to pull me closer. But this attempt at a desire that would never exist made me even more ashamed afterward, the pathetic realization that nothing had changed at all.

When I first began to inhabit Haddonfield in my imagination, I didn't know how soon the horrors that it represented so vividly would overlap with my own life. The on-screen murders were abstract to me, theoretical—symbolic of the kind of suffering I felt I deserved for what I was becoming. Those girls existed only so that Michael could kill them. Those dead girls weren't real. I could watch them be brutally slaughtered and then rewind the tape to the very beginning, bringing them back to life over and over again. But T had inhabited the edges of my own daily life, my life outside of Haddonfield, and her murder was a horror film that seemed to have been written just for me. I was the only person in an otherwise empty theater, my face lit up by the screen. I had to know what happened next.

I could have easily been watching Michael cross the lawn toward Laurie, who awaited her fate at his hands, when T was stabbed for the first time by her assailant. When she realized with dawning horror that she wasn't going to survive the night, I could have been watching Michael descend a staircase or stand in a doorway with his head cocked to the side while he selected his next victim, always gripping the handle of a knife. When T clawed at her attacker's face in those last desperate moments, I might have been watching Dr. Loomis race up the stairs to the room where Michael stood fumbling with his mask and finally confront his patient after his intense search through that darkest of nights. I might have been looking out the window at all the other quiet houses and wondering whether anyone else was awake out there like me, or whether I was the only one tormented by something pursuing me relentlessly through the dark.

The stories I'd been reading and the films I'd been watching had finally caught up to me and tracked me down, just as Michael had made his way back to Haddonfield and saw Laurie standing outside his childhood home as if having waited for him the whole time he'd been away. Now I was the one whose story was about to begin. The horror was finally real.

I already knew about the girl who survived, the one who made it to the end. I knew about Laurie. But now I wanted to know what it was like to be the one who succumbed. My desire was stoked by shame and fueled by a craving to be wanted so desperately even for that. I wanted to be Annie, watched and stalked and hunted by Michael until he is alone with her in the dark garage. I wanted to be Lynda, fooled by Michael into thinking I was safe just before I noticed the knife in his hands. I'd always been the one watching from the shadows, but now I wanted a spotlight to shine down on me and have all those hungry eyes look my way. Because to me, T's death meant that someone had wanted her more than anything in the world.

The story of the dead girl in my own Haddonfield became my new fairy tale, the man in the mask stepping aside to make room for T.

～

One day during the week after T's murder, I stepped into the hallway in the middle of class with a bathroom pass I'd requested from my teacher after completing a quiz early. The muffled voices of teachers were barely audible behind the closed doors of the other classrooms, and I soon found myself standing in front of what had been T's locker.

It was decorated with flowers and the cards that many of us had made for her in art class, writing her name with Magic Marker in clumsy letters highlighted with smears of glitter. We'd scribbled notes about how much we missed her, how nothing would be the same without her. A cheaply framed photograph of T and her siblings was taped to the front of the locker, and whole bouquets of flowers had been affixed to the metal door that had been opened only that first day to remove anything her family might have wanted to keep. I don't know exactly when I decided to take something from the items that now constituted T's memorial, but my fingers were suddenly touching the flowers, cupping them in my hands like treasures.

I might have already known I would take one of the flowers for myself—the hallway would be empty and no one would see. But one moment I was running my fingers carefully along the petals, taking great care not to damage them, and suddenly I was rushing down the hall to my own locker, my palm bleeding from a thorn of the single white rose I'd plucked from a bouquet.

Later, after the last bell rang, I wrapped the rose in tissue paper and slipped it into my backpack so that no harm would come to it. At home I found a vase in the kitchen cabinet and cleaned it meticulously, rinsing out the dust before filling it with water from the sink and then gently dipping the rose inside. I took it upstairs to my room and placed it next to my computer screen, then stepped back to admire it. I imagined it having been an offering from a boy who had loved T more than anything, a secret admirer now grieving her tragic loss. I painted a picture of him in my mind, this boy who pined for her even after she was gone forever, who had touched my rose before it was mine. He would be someone who had loved her from afar, too nervous and self-conscious to get too close. He would have a shy smile that he flashed when she looked his way, a pulse that quickened every time she entered the room.

I imagined him wanting me that way too. At night I pretended that he had meant the whole time for me to have the rose instead. It had been so easy to take it from her.

~

The dead girl has to die before the story about her can begin. She presents a mystery to be solved and offers the beginning of a story that will necessarily unfold in her absence. In *Twin Peaks*, a TV show I remember classmates at school talking about around the time of T's death, Laura Palmer's body washes up on a lonely beach wrapped in plastic, abandoned in the night and discovered early the next morning. In a tape recording she'd made before the events that led to her death, Laura says, "I just know I'm gonna get lost in those woods again tonight." It's up to Agent Cooper to interpret just what she means and ultimately venture into the woods himself.

The dead girl shows us that everything is not as it seemed. The story that begins with the discovery of her body often becomes a story about the man tasked with solving the mystery of her death, rooting out the how and the why. I understood myself as an investigator of T's murder in the week following the news of her death, if only in the version of her story that rapidly played out in my mind. As the vague and increasingly horrifying details about what happened the night she was killed slowly became known, I began to fill in the gaps with my imagination, fantasizing about all the ways in which it might have taken place.

Sometimes she had a secret boyfriend, a man she hadn't even told her friends about. Much older than we were at the time, maybe even a student at the college where she had been found. I pictured him with piercings and a tattoo, something tribal flashing across his shoulder and chest that she would lightly trace with her fingertips when he pulled off his shirt. He smoked cigarette after cigarette, holding them between thin fingers as he cupped her hands to light one for her as well. Stubble across his cheeks that he never bothered to shave. He picked her up on Saturday nights in an old sports car, maybe his father's old car, the car his father had driven girls around in when he himself was a beautiful young man. T's boyfriend drove fast down the highway with the windows rolled down, and she loved the sound of the music he played when he parked in empty lots and beckoned for her to climb across the gear shift to be even closer to him, pressing her body against his as the windows fogged up and they imagined they were completely alone in the world, greedily exploring each other's bodies in the dark. There was no one else but the two of them.

When I wondered what might have driven him to do it, I imagined a lover's quarrel. He had wanted her to run away with him to start a new life somewhere else. Maybe he'd gotten into some trouble, something dangerous he needed to get away from fast in the dead of night. He wanted to keep her with him no matter what, no matter where he had to go next. He loved her that much. But when she refused to leave with him, claiming she was too young to leave home or that she didn't imagine a future like that with someone like him, he couldn't keep his anger and hurt inside.

I'd seen violence like that in my father's house, and I tried to imagine T's boyfriend in the moment just after he realized he'd lost her. The way his face would turn ugly, his eyes like daggers, the strength in his body somehow doubled by the rage rapidly building up deep inside of him.

In other fantasies, he was a stranger. He picked her out from a crowd, watching her from a safe distance before following her home. I used to go with my mother to outdoor concerts at county fairs or free events in local parks, the adults cracking open beers snatched from coolers on wheels that had been dragged to a blanket somewhere in view of the stage. I would wander alone through the crowd as night fell, getting myself lost among the carnival booths and snack stands as all those colored lights brightened the sky above me. My mother would have given me enough money to play some of the arcade games and to buy a pretzel and a soda before I was expected to find my way back to her. On those nights I would imagine being watched and noticed and followed along the dark walkways between carnival stands, wondering if someone had singled me out from all the others. I would meet the gaze of men passing by and imagine a hint of desire or danger in their eyes, relishing the sense that anything at all could happen.

Maybe T's killer had seen her at a concert or in the park, a place where he could have easily seen me walking just ahead of her. Or maybe she'd been lounging in her swimsuit on a towel in her yard on an unseasonably hot day, her skin oily with suntan lotion and the direction of her gaze obscured by the sunglasses covering her eyes. Then he watched her afterward, perhaps even for days, following her and recording everything she did to memory. Making a plan for when he would make his move.

He watched her get off the school bus from inside a car that he had parked within view of her house to wait patiently for this very moment to come. He watched her from the dark of early evening through her bedroom window, which would have been lit up like something you could see from space. She danced around her bed and swayed from side to side in front of a mirror to music he couldn't hear, while he imagined it for himself as he watched her in silence. He watched as she wrote in a diary that she kept locked with a key on a necklace that she never took off, and he was so desperate to know her private thoughts that he felt the need deep in his bones, in the blood pumping through his veins—in the strength that he suddenly felt surging from his mind through his body to his fists. He wanted her to invite him inside. And then one Saturday night he saw her standing alone on the porch looking out into the neighborhood with boredom masking her otherwise beautiful face, and he finally got up the nerve to climb out of his car and make himself known.

I wanted to be watched just like T. Sometimes I stood at my bedroom window in the new house with the lights shining brightly behind me so that I was completely visible to the outside world, and when I looked at my own reflection in the glass, I imagined that I was being intently watched by someone standing just on the other side. I waited for his hand to press hard against the window to show me how badly he needed me. I waited for the window to shatter and for him to climb inside the room, shaking the broken glass onto the carpeted floor. Perhaps he would be holding up a jagged edge with his bare hands, angled and sharp, ready to stop me if I tried to run. But I would have given myself to him like something I no longer wanted, or something I'd been saving for a moment just like that one to come.

I knew that T hadn't asked for any of what happened to her, and I wished more than anything I'd been there instead of her. I wanted to finally get what I knew I deserved.

~

My mother had met her new boyfriend at the bar where she was still bartending a few nights each week. He'd become a regular, he and his friends knocking back beers at the end of the counter where my mother

97

stood taking orders, and he finally asked her on a date after working up his nerve over time. Later he hired her to do his company's bookkeeping so she could quit the job at the bar. He didn't want her spending her nights with all those other men.

My brother and I met S for the first time on a hot weekend afternoon that we spent out on a small lake in a fishing boat. One of S's friends steered the boat slowly through the water toward the best fishing spot while S and my mother sat together across from us on a padded bench. My mother clutched a plastic cup full of pink wine, and S sipped from a bottle of beer while my brother and I squinted into the sunlight and hovered over the edge of the boat with our fishing rods, waiting for something to bite. Earlier, S had shown us how to pierce the worm with the hook to make sure that it wouldn't come loose when the fish made a grab for it. He was older than my mother, his thick beard already going gray on the sides. He had a patient way of explaining how the fishing rods worked, and he raised his beer in my direction when I finally hauled up a catch from the depths.

S worked in construction and had a house on the other side of the county from ours, and my brother and I began spending long weekend afternoons and evenings there with him and our mother. He had a pool table in the basement where he taught me how to properly hold a cue. His two sons, both several years older than us, were always out with girls. They were star athletes whose soccer games we would attend on cool nights at the high school field, watching from bleachers where I'd stare openly at the boys pulling up the hems of their jerseys to wipe the sweat from their brows, their shorts sometimes riding high up their legs after a kick and clinging tightly around their muscled thighs.

We had stayed with S for a few months while our new house was being built after we sold the townhouse to make the down payment. The younger of S's two boys once barged into the room I was temporarily sharing with my brother and caught me playing with some small dolls I'd collected at the time, cheap off-brand plastic female figures that came with a variety of interchangeable outfits and accessories that I would use to stage elaborate scenes in a house I'd made for them with an old cardboard shoebox. I remember scrambling to put them all away even as he began pointing and laughing and rushing out of the room to tell his older brother what I'd been doing.

98

My mother and S joined a bowling league soon after they began dating. At first my brother and I would tag along while they closed down
the bar after the games were over, disappearing through a saloon door
and leaving us to play pinball and eat candy from a vending machine,
my mother handing over the quarters she received as change after each
new drink she ordered. In the men's restroom I discovered that through
a crack in the wall of a stall I had a clear view of the long line of urinals.
Sometimes I would sit on the toilet seat and sneak glances while the men
pissed and cracked jokes with each other, holding themselves in loose
fists with their bottles of beer in the other hand, never knowing I was
there. Never knowing I could see everything.

I especially enjoyed watching certain men, men who lingered at the
urinal or whose bodies I'd become most drawn to while watching them
on the lanes with their wives. I would scamper into the restroom if I saw
one of them headed in its direction, taking my place in the stall just in
time to watch him unzip his fly and pull himself out of his jeans. Sometimes those same men—S's friends from as far back as high school—
would clap me on my shoulder before we walked back to the car with our
mother at the end of the night, their eyes red-rimmed from too many
beers, fumbling with the keys to their pickup trucks. There would always
be a gruffness to the touch of their calloused hands, a sort of manly exchange of affection, and I wondered with a surge of almost giddy pleasure what they would be capable of doing to me if they ever found out
what I'd seen, ripping me apart limb from limb while I laughed until my
body could no longer make any sounds at all.

Eventually my brother and I were old enough to stay at S's house near
the bowling alley until he and my mother came back home from the bar.
We would be left to entertain ourselves on those long Saturday nights
while waiting for them, my mother buzzed and giggly and smelling of
the cigarettes they'd both been chain-smoking while bowling and drinking the night away. They always brought us drive-through fast food that
we would all devour together beneath the harsh and bright overhead
lights in the kitchen before they made their way unsteadily to bed, my
brother and I unfolding sheets and blankets and spreading them out on
the two living room couches before turning out the lights.

I never complained about these nights away from our own house
because S had the luxury of cable television, which we would never have

been able to afford at home, an endless stream of channels to click through. My brother would be playing video games downstairs in the basement on the consoles that S's older boys had outgrown, and I was able to sit alone in front of the TV in the living room with the lights off and explore everything it had to offer. I watched action films where men with ripped T-shirts and dirty faces wisecracked their way toward rescuing beautiful women who had found themselves in danger. I watched old reruns of classic shows I'd never known even existed.

The blocked pornography channels were just fuzzy scribbles of light and strange distortions, but sometimes the audio came through and I would listen quietly to the invisible adults making exaggerated sounds of passion and desire, moans and gasps and bodies colliding with more and more fervor, picturing in my mind's eye what exactly was bringing them so much pleasure. I imagined a nude woman on top of a shirtless man with her head thrown back, her face a mask of what could be either agony or ecstasy. A man holding a woman down with his hand over her mouth so she couldn't speak or cry out even if she'd wanted to. A woman touching men who were standing on either side of her naked body where she was splayed out on a large bed with fancy pillows and a curtain on either side, both of them pressing in toward her on their knees.

Maybe even two men kissing each other in the dark, their bare torsos pressed up against each other and letting no light through.

~

Only a single week had passed since T's murder when my mother drove us the half hour down the highway toward S's house for another Saturday bowling night, another night I would spend in front of the TV scrolling through the channels until something caught my eye.

T's killer had not yet been identified, and the fact that he was still out there was all anyone was talking about at school. There had been a memorial assembly earlier in the week during which her best friends spoke briefly into a microphone while a slideshow of photographs was projected onto a screen behind them. The girls on stage were fighting back tears as they repeated over and over again how nice T had been to them. Everyone said how much fun it had been to be around her, to bathe in her glow. She was praised for her charisma and her obvious beauty. Her adorable laugh, her gleaming smile. And as the photographs appeared one by one before us in the audience, no one could take their eyes off her. I was obsessively watching the nightly news that week for any mention of T. And as my mother exited the highway on that Saturday night before we would make our way through the winding residential streets toward S's house, I suddenly saw a sign indicating the location of the college campus where T's body had been found. I sat up straight in my seat, eyes wide and searching.

I'd passed the campus many times before in my mother's car without even realizing what it was. I'd seen students walking the same wooded pathways that T had walked with her eventual killer as we approached S's house each week. The bowling alley where my mother spent those Saturday nights was practically adjacent to the front lawn of the campus, just a short drive around the corner and up a hill overlooking the brown brick buildings dotting the grounds from where the winding sidewalk running alongside a small stream intersected with pathways like the one where T had been found. Police cars were everywhere, and I saw that the whole area was cordoned off from the public, closed at that moment even to the students who were finishing up the spring semester.

We had to take a detour just to get back to the main road. My mother was going to be late. She was muttering under her breath, pale fingers tapping the steering wheel in frustration as we inched forward. But while we waited to be ushered past the crime scene by the police officer standing in the middle of the road directing traffic with a neon baton, my mother grumbling and glancing anxiously at the digital clock on the dashboard, I pressed my face to the passenger-side window and tried to catch a glimpse of something new to add to the story I'd been mentally writing about what had happened to T. But all I saw was a dimming twilight, a familiar darkness descending in the distance.

Then I thought back to the week before. I'd already been dropped off at S's house—after seeing my father in the park—when T was murdered, just a short walk from where it had happened. The man who chose her could have chosen me instead, if only he'd known I was there. If only he'd seen me first.

~

That night, during my perpetual scrolling through the channel directory after my brother and I were left alone in the house, I happened upon an old slasher film featuring teenagers running through a dark campground while moonlight shimmers on the surface of a lake in the distance, and

I was immediately brought back to those afternoons at my father's house where I'd obsessively watched *Halloween*. I realized that I was once again in a town just like Haddonfield, the tree-lined streets outside the window at S's house easily imagined into the world where Michael Myers prowled the sidewalks at night. A town where a murder had been committed and where a killer still walked the streets.

He could be anyone outside, walking past the living room window at that very moment, looking in for his next victim. I peered out through the glass and imagined I could see someone just like Michael lurking in the hedgerows just past the covered swimming pool, hiding among the thick branches of the bushes lining the fence or maybe standing perfectly still in one of the neighbors' yards that I could barely see from my vantage point. I wondered whether other victims were out there whose bodies had yet to be discovered, waiting silent and bloody and ruined in a dark and otherwise empty house.

I might have even heard police sirens in the distance sounding the alarm.

Just before her final confrontation with Michael Myers, Laurie Strode crosses the street to the Wallace house to check on her friends. She stands on the porch with her brow furrowed, unnerved by the dark and the quiet. The only light comes from the candle inside the jack-o'-lantern on the front porch. After ringing the doorbell and calling out to her friends by name, Laurie circles around the house and enters through the back door. The light from the streetlamp throws sharp angles against the interior walls of the house, revealing the myriad places in which someone could be lying in wait. The landing upstairs is entirely dark except at the far end of the hall where a long and slanted beam of light on the carpeted floor comes from a door that is slightly ajar. Laurie's body as she walks down the hallway is just a dark and shapeless mass until her face becomes partially illuminated as she pushes open the door, and then her hands fly to her face in horror when she sees Annie's corpse splayed across the bed, a headstone stolen from Michael's dead sister's grave now lodged crudely behind the pillows.

Laurie's sobs are muffled as she stumbles to the side, grasping at a wall for support just as Bob's suspended body swings down from the darkness of a doorway behind her. She releases a bloodcurdling scream when an adjacent cabinet door slides open to reveal the wide-eyed face of Lynda's corpse. Laurie has only a moment to spare in her shock and horror before Michael makes his presence known, his masked face barely discernible behind her in the shadows. The conclusion to the film in which Michael relentlessly pursues Laurie through the dark passageways of her waking nightmare unfolds in a series of sudden confrontations and close calls.

That night at S's house I imagined what it would be like to walk through the dark rooms behind me and find the bodies of my own loved ones. My mother and S would have been the first victims, never having made it to the bowling alley, then my brother in the basement, where I thought he was still happily playing video games and never noticed that the sound effects downstairs had been abruptly silenced.

And my father. He was there, too, that night in the horror film of my mind, but he wouldn't have survived the walk down the long hallway. He would have crumpled to the ground just like anyone else as I passed him by.

I stood up from the couch and walked slowly out of the living room, through the kitchen and into the hallway leading to the foyer, stopping only when I arrived at the locked front door. T had been found only a mile away the week before, and I didn't yet know that her killer had been identified that very night—the reason for the surge of activity at the crime scene as we took the detour earlier—and that he would be found and arrested before dawn in a motel just over the river from where I sat and imagined myself once more into Haddonfield.

I reached toward the lock on the front door leading out to the porch and the darkness of the world beyond, and I gently slid the deadbolt to the side with a barely audible click. Now the door was open. Whoever might be waiting out there could freely come inside.

My pulse quickened as I took one step back into the foyer, and then another and another still, my gaze fixed on the newly unlocked door. Anything could happen now. The door could fling wildly open and Michael could be standing there, knife in hand and ready for the pursuit. Or he could trick me and come in from the back patio while I was staring at the front door, not realizing he'd been watching me the whole time and had already anticipated the ways in which I might behave.

All I could hear was the rush of blood through my body, a violent pulsing behind my skin that demanded to finally be heard.

9

I'D BEEN GETTING CLOSER AND CLOSER to the man at the end of the long hallway whom I still dreamed about most nights, slipping into my slow march midstride, as if part of me was always making the interminable walk toward whatever fate awaited me. The deaths of the people in the dream were becoming more grotesque. Sometimes they would dismember themselves before dealing the killing blow with the knife or the maul, body parts strewn on the path before me that I had to step past carefully or else I would trip and fall into a growing pool of blood. One man would hack away at his arms and legs until he could no longer hold the blade. Then he would crumple to the ground, his gaze locked on mine.

By then I was almost able to recognize each of their faces as they fell. Something in their eyes looked eerily familiar, the way the characters Dorothy encounters in Oz bear a striking resemblance to the people she knows in the real world. But I still couldn't stop myself from walking forward. I couldn't stop making them do it. The path behind me was riddled with corpses, and I knew that more would die before I reached the end, but I still couldn't stop walking. Not until I saw who was waiting for me.

~

At school that Monday morning, everyone was talking about the killer.

I stepped down onto the curb from the school bus and saw a group of kids in my grade huddled together by the flagpole and talking excitedly about what part of the story they'd been told. One of the boys raised his hand and clenched his fist as though he held a knife, and then his arm came crashing down again and again into the middle of the circle, the girls to either side of him pretending to scream in horror and then laughing nervously, glancing around to check whether anyone else had seen.

The boy arrested for T's murder had been discovered hiding out in a cheap hotel room on Saturday night on the other side of the river from where I'd sat up late at S's house unable to sleep, waiting for the front door to fly open and for the man with the knife to be standing at the ready, greedily running his tongue over his lips before he stepped inside. I would learn much later in reports from the trial that T had been babysitting her younger siblings at her mother's boyfriend's apartment on the night she was killed, just as Laurie had been doing with Tommy and Lindsey in Haddonfield. She'd been less than a mile from where S lived when her killer had singled her out, and where I'd sat quietly alone in the dark on the night she'd been murdered, not knowing how close I was to witnessing what was happening to her. The night I'd been replaying in my imagination ever since.

The boy who killed her had seen her smoking a cigarette on the front porch of the building, and he'd somehow coaxed her away to walk the short distance to his dorm room at the college. He said in court he'd lured her there with a juice box, like something I would have stowed in my cooler on those long Saturdays after my mother dropped me off at my father's house.

I pictured the two of them lying side by side on his bed, music drifting around their tense and nervous bodies, the light of a desk lamp casting shadows on the freshly painted walls. His body beside her on the bed was warm. The hand lightly grazing hers was gentle, and the lyrics of the songs he played were like a secret message meant only for her. He finally offered to walk her home, back to where her younger siblings were waiting for her to return. But she would never make it there. Somewhere along the footpath, T and the boy who had pursued her stopped next to a water tower to smoke one last cigarette, and he later said that that was the moment he knew he was going to kill her—when he finally saw exactly how the night was going to end. I imagined the decision dawning on him like the solution to a math problem, all the pieces clicking suddenly into place.

The psychological evaluations all reported that he would have likely become a serial killer if he hadn't been caught after T's murder. He confessed that he'd been hunting for someone like her for a while.

He didn't look or act in a way that would mark him as unhinged or unfit for society. No blight on his face to give him away, no evidence on his body indicating the violence he was capable of committing. I stared at his photograph in the newspaper and studied it for hidden clues, something wrong about him that only I would be able to detect, just as I'd often stared at my own face in the bathroom mirror in search of something that would give me away. It was later said that he had a history of looking. He'd lived in a mobile home community with his mother and sister until the management company kicked them out because he had been caught peeping into the bedroom windows of young girls. He was someone who watched from the shadows—someone who looked.

The boy by the flagpole had turned suddenly in my direction as I walked toward the front doors of the school. He was still holding the imaginary knife, his raised hand in a fist.

~

One of the final confrontations between Laurie and Michael takes place in a closet. Laurie cowers on the floor in the shadows beneath some shirts hanging above her head as Michael's shadow almost completely blocks the only light coming through the slats of the closet door. Methodically tracing its contours with the blade of his knife, he begins to struggle with the door while Laurie moans quietly and helplessly from the floor, her knees pulled to her chest, any trace of hope draining from her terrified face as Michael hacks through the slats and begins to grope blindly for her inside the closet.

The light suddenly flashes on and Michael's face looms above her, low grunts emanating from behind the plastic mask. In a moment of quick thinking, Laurie hastily fashions one of the wire hangers into a weapon. Michael has by now forced his way almost completely inside the closet as the light goes off again, and when he becomes disarmed by the sudden darkness, she takes the opportunity to jab the hanger up toward his mask. She manages to stab him in the eye, and he drops his knife as he recoils in pain. Laurie is then able to grab the sharper weapon and stab him properly, and he falls to the floor.

Michael has watched Laurie throughout the film from a variety of vantage points, and in the act of stabbing him in the eye—the only vulnerable part of his face because of the mask—she is punishing him for his looking. I knew when I saw her do it that I should have been punished too. All those boys I'd watched at the swimming pool and the locker room, and then the boy in my father's old neighborhood. Those men at the bowling alley who never knew I was there.

I knew what I'd been doing was wrong. But I still didn't know how to stop.

~

The school year ended a couple months after T's killer was caught, and I began spending my days at a camp that my brother and I had attended for the past several summers. The camp was a sprawling, largely un-touched wooded wilderness nestled between the boundaries of several suburban developments in a larger town closer to the city. The counsel-ors arranged various activities for the campers, posting the day's calendar on a bulletin board every morning. Kickball games, dodgeball, obstacle courses, arts and crafts, sessions at the large swimming pool spaced out for each age group. I was still reliving the details about T's death in my mind, and I spent most of my time alone wandering the fields and get-ting lost in the woods, thinking at length about what her final moments might have been like. My thirteenth birthday would take place near the end of the summer, marking the beginning of my adolescence. The boys my age were developing muscles in places that used to be flat and smooth, and I would sneak glances at them while we changed into our swim-suits and then watch them in the pool as they pulled themselves up out of the water after each dive from the diving board. I cataloged every inch of their exposed skin with my eyes, my mind building a careful archive of their changing bodies.

I had also become hopelessly enamored with one of the male coun-selors, a recent high school graduate with light brown hair that fell like a cresting wave across his forehead and a sexy, inviting smile that seemed always to contain a secret joke. Something he would tell me if we could ever be alone together. He'd caught my eye on the first day that summer, hopping down from the door of a busload of kids from another town. His tight khaki shorts, cinched loosely with a brown leather belt, revealed the thickness of his thighs and taut calf muscles. He quickly became the most popular counselor at camp, and I remember him always being surrounded by an entourage, girls shyly watching his every move and boys boisterously trying to impress him with their wit or their athleti-cism, instinctively trying to gain his approval.

There was a game of dodgeball behind the pavilion just a couple weeks into the camp session, and I had signed up only because I saw this counselor's name next to the activity listing. I stood in the half-circle of boys as the game was about to begin, each of us holding a red rubber ball between our palms, and one by one we took our turn dodging the onslaught from our peers, our eyes cast furtively to the sides like cornered animals until the inevitable strike marked the end of our turn. My aim was good, and I glanced at the counselor each time I landed a shot to make sure he'd noticed.

Eventually it was my turn to dodge, and I reluctantly took my place surrounded by boys poised with their rubber balls, shifting their weight from side to side as they sized me up. I successfully dodged the first few throws, leaping to the side as I sensed a toss headed my way. I liked the whoosh of air in front of my face after a narrow miss, the other boys cursing under their breath as they scrambled to pick up their ball for another throw. I tossed my body back and forth in the circle as the balls came at me faster and harder as something changed in the faces of my opponents, their eyes narrowing with each missed attempt to take me down.

I'd lasted longer than any of them. I was making them angry. The game had now changed into something else entirely.

A ball finally made contact and bounced lightly off my shoulder, and with a mixture of disappointment and relief I thought the game was over. I caught the eye of the counselor as he was about to call the game in favor of the boy who'd thrown the ball that had made contact. But then the throws kept coming, harder now because I wasn't dodging anymore. I shielded my face and screamed for them to stop. Each landed blow was accompanied by a shout as the ball bounced hard off my body. "Get him!" someone said, laughing.

I tried to push my way out of the game, but the boys pressed their shoulders together so I couldn't get through. Finally I curled up into a ball on the ground, the balls bouncing off my back and shoulders and neck as the circle closed in around me. The shouts of the beautiful counselor were drowned out by the jeers of the other boys, but I finally felt strong hands on the sides of my arms, a shadow blocking out the sun. I recognized the camp's logo on his brown polo shirt before I realized it was the counselor himself who was enfolding me in his arms, protecting me and waving off the other boys who were losing interest now that he had intervened, the rubber balls all rolling to a stop around me.

"You're all suspended next period," the counselor said gruffly as he ordered the other boys back to the covered pavilion. Then it was just the two of us, my heavy breathing finally slowing as the counselor rubbed my shoulders and finally pulled me to my feet.

"You'll be okay," he said, flashing the smile that had made me immediately fall in love with him. "You know they're just jealous. Nothing could get you. You were the best player in the whole group."

I nodded vigorously, pulling my shoulders back and making my chest big. "I'm okay," I said. I could still feel the pressure of his palm on my neck, the smell of his shirt as it covered my face, his breath hot on my cheek as he scolded the other boys for mistreating me. "Thanks," I added, already searing the experience into memory, making it something I could call up again when I was alone in my bedroom in the dark. Or anytime I was afraid.

After that, I would sign up for all the activities next to that counselor's name on the schedule just to be close to him. I suffered through softball games where I missed even the easiest pitch just so I could watch his beautiful face squinting into the sunlight and have his eyes on me and me alone, however briefly. I would sit near him at lunchtime, close enough to smell the chlorine in his hair if he'd been in the pool or the sweat that had dried into the fabric of his T-shirt if he'd been running a game of kickball beneath the hot early summer sun. I would laugh the loudest of all when he made a joke. I would laugh until he looked my way, laugh and laugh until I was sure he'd noticed.

One morning I was called to the main office over the loudspeaker for a meeting with the camp director, the eyes of the other campers all turning my way as my name rang out. The director was an older woman with a bronze face creased and tightened by too much time in the sun. She reminded me of a park ranger in her light brown vest. Everyone was afraid of her because it seemed as if she existed only to dole out punishment, and I'd never been called to meet with her before. I didn't realize she even knew my name until I heard it coming from the speakers mounted in all four corners of the pavilion, my face reddening from the shame of already knowing I'd done something wrong.

I walked slowly into the director's office after everyone had dispersed for the first session of activities, and she told me to sit down in a metal folding chair in front of a desk covered with papers—attendance sheets, notes from parents, permission slips. She asked me how my summer was going so far and whether I was enjoying myself at camp. I nodded without saying anything, averting my gaze and staring instead at the wooden floorboards beneath my feet. But when she mentioned the counselor I loved by name, I somehow knew what she was going to say next.

"You need to stop following him around so much," said the director, her hands folded patiently on the desk in front of her like this was something she always had to explain to boys like me. In my memory she's squinting at me when she says it, and I'm much smaller than I actually was at the time, shrinking farther into the chair with each word she says. She looms over me and casts a long shadow.

"You need to sign up for activities with the other counselors too," she continued. "I know you're fond of him, but you can't be around him all the time. It's not right."

I'd somehow imagined that I'd been invisible the whole time and that no one could tell how much I wanted to be near him. No one had seen me follow him with my eyes, lingering just a few steps behind him on the way back to the pavilion, lightly grazing his hand as I slipped past him to retrieve my lunch from the cooler in my cubby. But now I knew I'd been a fool. I cringed inwardly as I remembered each pathetic moment in turn. And I wondered if the director herself had been the one to notice, whether any of the papers on the desk beneath her wrinkled outstretched hands might be a detailed list of every time she'd caught me staring at him or following him or scrawling his name with a twig in the sandbox at the corner of the playground when I thought no one could see. And then I realized with increasing horror that he himself might have noticed that he'd caught a dangerous kind of attention from me and then reported me for my misguided affection. Maybe he'd been disgusted by me and couldn't stand the sight of me anymore.

"He's such a creep," I imagined him saying to the other counselors at lunchtime. "He's not normal. He shouldn't be around the other boys— not the way he is."

In the days that followed my meeting with the camp director, I spent even more time alone. Before my love of the counselor had taken root,

I used to wander as far as possible from the camp buildings through the woods each day, slinking far enough away from where the other children were playing to where I could no longer hear their chatter and shouts and calls to each other across the playgrounds and ball fields. I would always be surprised when I suddenly pushed through a bend of trees and came upon the backyards of the large suburban houses just past the tree line. I ran my fingers along the chain-link fences as I walked down the row of houses, all the backyards quiet and empty. Electric grills and trampolines and above-ground swimming pools bordered by colorful flower gardens all sat dormant and exposed in the sunlight. During those long afternoons at camp, waiting for the day to finally be over, I spent my time alone, imagining what might be tucked away inside those houses. All those dark hallways and empty rooms. I sometimes made half-hearted plans to infiltrate them, imagining how long I would lie in wait until someone found me hiding inside.

After the morning in the director's office, I began to return to the empty houses, leaving the camp area during open play periods and wandering alone through the trees. Over time I learned the way through the woods that would get me to the houses most quickly, forging a path I made sure not to wear down too much so that no one would ever know where I'd been when I later emerged from the woods. I would sit in the grass next to the backyard fences beneath the hot summer sun, reading my mother's paperback novels, daydreaming about the counselor who had betrayed me, and waiting to go back to my own house, my own empty room. I no longer dared to even look at the counselor I'd loved, knowing he could see right through me to the rotten core I'd tried for so long to hide.

At some point during those long afternoons, someone in one of those houses must have seen me through a window that to me reflected only the summer sunlight. Someone would have noticed me while doing dishes or having a snack at the kitchen table. I wonder what they thought about the lonely boy emerging from the woods each day to see what he might find among those who lived at its edge. I wonder if they ever considered inviting me inside. I wonder if they thought I needed help— or if they thought of calling someone to take me away and out of their sight for good.

10

WE TOOK A FAMILY VACATION TO FLORIDA that summer to a beachside town an hour north of Miami that's now etched impossibly bright in my memory like the afterimage of a sunburst. My mother and brother and me, along with S and his two older sons. He must have been the one to suggest the plan to my mother, because we had never considered traveling before, the expense too great to even warrant a discussion. Late June, the days already long and heavy. I welcomed the chance to escape summer camp for the week, and I spent the days before the trip fantasizing about the ocean, imagining the smell of salty air and the sound of waves crashing onto the sand.

My father called the house on the morning we left as I was gathering the last of the things that I wanted to take with me, but his voice was already slurring when he said my name. I hung up the phone without saying goodbye and continued packing my suitcase in silence.

We drove all night and into the next day in a rented minivan, through Missouri into Kentucky and then down into Tennessee and Georgia. Just after dawn, a green sign welcomed us into Florida and the vast black expanse of night eventually gave way to morning. The swamplands alongside the highway looked to me like the surface of another planet, something from the old pulp science fiction paperbacks that lined my grandfather's bookshelves—shirtless and muscular men on the covers battling giant reptiles in otherworldly rainforests. The heat seeped in through the windows despite the air conditioning being on full blast, and I pressed my face to the glass, counting down the mile markers.

We were almost there.

My mother and S had taken turns at the wheel, staying awake by guzzling coffee purchased from roadside gas stations while the other slept in the passenger seat, my mother's head bobbing lightly forward toward the windshield with each touch of the brakes while S was driving. I didn't take my eyes off the window even for a minute as the world passed by all night in the deep darkness stretching out from the highway toward the dim lights of distant towns that I would never see up close. I spent those hours picturing boat rides at sunset, the line of the horizon visible from every window of our room at the resort, swimming pools with water more clear and blue than any I had ever seen. My mother had shown me a brochure for the sprawling beachside complex where we would be staying, and I instantly fell in love with the tropical fantasy evoked by the oversaturated images. Palm trees and seashells, the sunrise each morning like a huge and beautiful wave cresting just as it reached the shoreline.

I'd been to Florida once before, with my father. He had flown my brother and me down to Tampa with him not long after the divorce on airline miles he'd earned while traveling for one of his short-lived jobs as the manager of a restaurant at the airport. It was my first time up in the air, and from my window seat I couldn't believe how small everything looked down below. We stayed at a cheap hotel with a central courtyard with a pool and a hot tub, and we didn't leave the hotel the entire time we were there. We never saw anything but the inside of a taxi from the airport and then the interior of a small room with a foldout couch and a double bed I shared with my brother. I remember once asking my father if we could go to the beach, which I'd fully expected to see when he announced the trip. And he told me we would, but we never did. My father drank beer after beer the entire time we were there, and he was mostly passed out by early afternoon either in the hotel room or in a chair by the pool. Meanwhile I swam alone in the deep end or splashed around doing underwater gymnastics with my brother in the shallows until darkness fell and we ate cheap food from the snack bar for dinner before heading back to the room and watching TV until it was time for bed.

Sometimes I just floated on my back in the pool while watching the sky for hours at a time. We flew home two days after we had arrived.

But I knew this time was going to be different. And when we finally pulled up to the parking lot of the resort and stepped out of the van after the long drive, stretching our legs in the thick humidity that made my skin clammy and fogged up the lenses of the glasses I'd begun wearing earlier that year, I knew I was going to have the time of my life. I was going to see the ocean. I was going to dive into a wave taller than I was, and I'd be swept beneath it into salty water that had traveled all the way from another continent, some foreign and faraway place, just to wash ashore where I'd been waiting this whole time to see it.

I remember arriving at the resort as if it was the beginning of a film, the anticipation about what was still to come almost more than I could bear. The camera has been following the van down the highway during the opening credits, the blue waters of the ocean reflecting the bright sunlight in the distance. In my mind the shot is like the opening sequence of Stanley Kubrick's adaptation of Stephen King's *The Shining*, the Torrance family's yellow car shot from above and behind as they drive through the mountains toward the Overlook Hotel. The Florida resort is then revealed to the viewer in a sweeping overhead shot, a sprawling maze of pathways through lush, dense greenery, with thick clusters of palm trees opened up to the sky. Waves lap lazily onto a mound of sand on a crowded beach. Sunbathers lie beside a pool filled with impossibly blue water, towel boys in white shirts rushing busily in and out of thatched huts. Shirtless teenage boys are engaged in a heated competition on a shuffleboard court. Small heads are bobbing above the water in a bubbling hot tub. Everything is so bright you almost have to shield your eyes.

And then a slow zoom to the parking lot where a young boy just twelve years old climbs awkwardly out of the back seat of the van and squints hard in the sudden bright light. Only now do we see his body and his face. He's not like I remembered, or at least he's not how I remember feeling at the time when I pictured how I might look to others. This boy's limbs are lanky and taut like a rope pulled tight, but not so grotesquely skinny and fragile and vulnerable like the boy I saw in my reflection in the mirror at the time. There are muscles lining his arms, and his legs would carry him fast if he needed to run. His watchful eyes are more curious than afraid, his gaze darting here and there as he takes everything in. The T-shirt he wears is too big for him, and he seems to be hiding inside it. When shopping for clothes at that age, I'd always imagined myself two sizes bigger than I really was, hoping somehow to fake my way into broader shoulders and a thicker chest. My blond hair is trimmed short on the sides, wavy bangs draped unevenly down over my forehead almost to my brow, which I swipe away with a practiced gesture that I probably imagined was casually masculine, like something a leading man would do in a movie.

While my mother and S checked us in at the front desk, both of them tired and irritable after the long drive, I wandered toward the glass wall separating the lobby from the pool area. In a film I would be shot from the outside with my face pressed close to the glass and my breath making little clouds of condensation spring up on the window. Then the camera would follow my eye line, revealing me to have been gazing not at the pool or toward the snack bar as the viewer might expect, but rather at the group of older boys heckling each other at the shuffleboard court, the tension in the muscles of their bare backs as they each take their turn. You can tell how badly I want them by the way my eyes narrow and my fist slowly clenches as I become transfixed by their every move.

At this moment the soundtrack would be cued, low and hypnotic notes that are meant to inspire the onset of either desire or dread. You can't tell yet which one it will be.

My mother eventually pulled me away from the window and asked me to help unload the van. "There will be time for that later," she said without knowing what exactly had captured my attention, and I stole one last glance at the boys at the shuffleboard court before following her back outside, the sun hot on my pale skin. We rolled the old suitcases borrowed from my grandparents down a narrow concrete pathway and then dragged them up a single flight of stairs to an open-air corridor that led to doors leading into the various suites. I was too excited to unpack my things once we got inside. The sun was going to set soon. I wanted to see everything before it got dark.

"I promise I won't go far," I said as I stood next to the suitcase containing my clothes and swim gear, a few paperbacks I'd brought to read on the beach.

My mother was holding a bright green swimsuit up to her body with the tags still on it, little yellow flowers drawn across the chest. She sighed and said, "Fine. But get back here before it gets dark. We'll all drive down the road for dinner. I saw a place with a view of the water."

I scampered down the corridor and stairs away from the suite, raced past the laundry area, the vending machines, the service elevator, and the recycling bins, and finally entered the courtyard. My eyes were immediately drawn to the exposed flesh of the shirtless men loitering by the bar and the café or treading water in the deep end of the pool, toweling off next to lounge chairs where beautiful women wearing oversized sunglasses were reading romance novels or thumbing through the glossy pages of magazines. A sign pointed toward the resort's private beach, and I walked quickly down a narrow concrete passageway covered in sand that guests had tracked in, almost slipping in my cheap plastic sandals as I hurried down the ramp. I could hear the ocean before I could see it—the low murmur of waves crashing gently on the shoreline. And then the distant horizon over the open sea was revealed to me for the first time.

I saw children splashing in the water and putting finishing touches on sandcastles destined to be swept away when the tide came in, a game of beach volleyball, girls in bikinis jumping into the air and slapping the ball back and forth, shirtless boys watching surreptitiously nearby, sipping sodas and jabbing each other playfully in the ribs in response to jokes I couldn't hear. A family sitting nearby was tying up their umbrella and gathering towels and beach bags as they prepared to head back in for dinner. But in that moment I felt as if I was completely alone. The shot in the film would have blurred out everyone else, holding only my own face in focus as I gazed out over the open water.

I clutched my sandals in my hands and dug my toes deeper into the sand, the sky turning from blue to pink and then a deep orange before the sun finally dipped behind me. All I could see in the distance were the small white crests of gentle waves lapping toward me from the dark, yellow lights on the decks of boats anchored somewhere out there on the horizon as the sound of pop music drifted inland from one of the fancy yachts. If anyone had been watching me and taking note of this young boy who had just wandered onto the beach alone, I wouldn't have seen him at all—wouldn't have noticed anything but the paradise I'd just discovered. But now the camera pulls back and reveals a shadowy figure watching from the boardwalk whose eyes we've actually been seeing through for the entire time the boy has been there, his singular focus foreshadowing whatever is going to happen next.

I waited until I couldn't see past the dark shoreline in the distance before finally turning around and walking back to the suite, the lights of the resort all ablaze before me.

~

I spent the first slow days of the trip wandering from the beach to the pool to the hot tub and back again, always watching the other guests at the resort, my eyes adjusting like a camera trained from afar. I watched from the small balcony overlooking the courtyard around the swimming pool and the hot tub. I watched from the stone pathways that I wandered alone, mapping the grounds of the resort to memory. I watched during my walks up and down the beach, the water gliding over my feet as I sorted through a collection of seashells that I planned to take home and pass around at summer camp as evidence of where I'd been, everyone's eyes burning with jealousy as they saw me display them.

Just up the beach from the resort there was a long pier where I'd slip underneath and look up between the wooden boards at people gazing out toward the horizon, no one ever knowing I was there—mostly teen-agers making out against the railing, a boy pressing against a girl while his hands roamed beneath her T-shirt or the beach towel she'd wrapped around her wet shoulders. I once saw a girl grab the front of a boy's swim shorts while he kissed her neck and cupped her face in his hands, the outline of his erection clearly visible just a few feet from where I was crouched beneath him.

S's sons fell in with a group of older kids who made bonfires on the beach at night and catcalled young women in bikinis sitting alone on towels during the day, laughing and cheering if she turned her head to look their way. My brother busied himself doing handstands in the shallow end of the pool and building sandcastles on the beach near my mother, who sat beneath an umbrella reading a mystery novel and sip-ping from a wine cooler while S napped on a chair beside her. I liked to be underwater in the deep end when the lights came on at dusk, the blue bottom of the pool lighting up like a stage. I'd emerge from below the surface and watch through the lenses of my goggles as the older boys took once again to the shuffleboard court, bronze and bare chested, cut-off shorts damp over tight swim shorts drying slowly as they played.

One early afternoon I went alone to the hot tub, leaving my mother and S lounging by the pool near the bar that served frozen drinks in plastic cups from colorful blenders, my mother's hands shiny from where the sludge had melted and slid down the side of the cup onto her fingers. My brother had gotten a bad sunburn halfway through the trip, so he was upstairs in the air-conditioned suite, small bubbles spreading across his sun-scorched back and shoulders even after my mother applied lotions and aloe and the other creams that the girl at the pharmacy had recommended. I walked the short distance toward the hot tub down a path lined with palm trees, skinny little lizards scuttling across the pavement at my feet, and I slipped quietly into the water after pressing the button to turn on the jets. The hot tub was large enough for maybe eight people, but it was completely unoccupied at first. I paddled around as the bubbles began to froth up to the surface, trying to find the spot with the most pressurized jet stream. And then I waited to see who would join me there.

A young couple eventually appeared and smiled politely at me before slipping into the water at the other end of the hot tub, and I pretended not to be listening while they talked about their dinner plans at the fancy restaurant overlooking the beach, both of them sipping from bottles of beer into which the man had first shoved lime wedges, the woman laughing as the juice sprayed her cheeks. She wore a black bikini that made her skin look even whiter than it really was, but even as I noticed that she was beautiful, someone whom S's older boys would have gawked at openly, my eyes were not drawn to her at all. The man was elegantly thin with a long and lean torso, his skin slightly reddened from too much time in the sun. He had an easy laugh, and the edges of his eyes crinkled when he smiled. He'd said hello to me as he slipped into the water, but I knew there was nothing I'd be able to say in response that wouldn't give me away, so I just smiled weakly and splashed my face with the bubbles frothing up around me. Sometimes he would grab at the woman beneath the surface of the water, and she would elicit a high-pitched squeal, feigning surprise as the bubbles disguised exactly where on her body his fingers had wandered.

He wore swim shorts snug around his midsection that had left little to my already wild imagination when I watched him step gingerly into the hot water.

Soon we were joined by another young couple and then two older men who I gathered had abandoned their wives to a shopping adventure and were enjoying the same frozen cocktails that my mother had been sipping when I'd left her over by the pool. The two men were sitting to my left, and the couple who had arrived first had gradually moved closer and closer to me as the others joined us so that I was finally sitting between the thin man with the beautiful smile and the more boisterous of the two men who had arrived last. All of us were arranged in a circle with just our heads and necks above the water while the jets shot against our backs and around our legs and feet, and I felt blissfully invisible as my legs began to lightly brush up against other legs beneath the water, some of them hairy and muscled, all of our feet and toes pushed against one another by the jets and by our movements in the water toward and away from the wall.

The adults were all talking to each other now, the booze having loosened their tongues. Favorite sports teams and restaurant recommendations, a souvenir shop off the beaten path where the women had bought summer dresses and cheap jewelry. I learned that the man whose knee I'd now allowed my own to rest heavily against was from Texas, and I pictured him wearing tight jeans and a cowboy hat, wiping his brow with a handkerchief he kept folded in his back pocket as he worked shirtless in a barn on a clear summer day, his chest hair slick with sweat.

And that was when I realized I was hard. The mesh underwear of my swimming trunks painfully constrained my erection as I tried to subtly adjust myself beneath the water, but then even the slightest touch sent shivers of ecstasy through my body, all the more thrilling because no one could tell what I was doing. No one could see. But I also hadn't realized how much my body temperature had been rising. I didn't even know how long I had been in the hot tub. I remembered reading the warnings on the signs next to the pressure adjustment knobs about the dangerous effects of staying in for too long. I would become dizzy. I would grow nauseous. I might faint. And suddenly I experienced all those symptoms coming on at once, but still my erection would not subside, and I couldn't stand up to leave because then everyone would know. I felt my face reddening by the minute, my breaths coming shorter and shorter and the fabric of my swimsuit still impossibly tight around my body. I had to control the panic rising in my chest, had to avoid drawing attention to myself. But it was becoming more and more difficult as I felt a sickness growing steadily inside of me.

Somehow I managed to wait until everyone had gotten out to go their separate ways before I crawled up the three steps to the footpath and then to the shade of the palm trees, my body hot and my skin shriveled and my head swimming around in choppy circles. I vomited suddenly and violently onto the ground, my knees digging into the concrete. A beer bottle was lodged into the ground next to the base of a palm tree, and discarded lime wedges were littered across the pathway. The sight made me remember the thin man in the hot tub, and even as I retched and trembled and then spat onto the ground until I could no longer taste my own bile, the memory of what had happened beneath the water came bubbling up again as if from a dream.

I'd been touched by the man with the beautiful smile. His body had met mine beneath the water, and he hadn't recoiled from the feeling of my skin against his own. And no one had ever told me to leave.

~

The only other time Michael Myers is unmasked in *Halloween*, after his father removes his clown mask at the end of the opening sequence, is by Laurie Strode herself. She has just stood up shakily from the hallway floor where she was recovering from the shock of her encounter with Michael in the closet, and she now believes that he's finally dead after she stabbed him with his own knife. But then he suddenly rises from the floor behind her. She doesn't even know that he has regained consciousness as he begins to walk methodically toward her just as she steps onto the landing at the top of the stairs. Laurie is alone in the frame for only a brief moment before Michael catches her from behind and turns her around to face him, his hands already at her throat.

He begins to choke her.

Laurie's panicked astonishment is palpable as she thrashes about within Michael's grip, and in all the commotion of the scene I thought she was likely grappling for his throat, perhaps trying to weaken his hold on her own. But then I saw that she's only trying to remove the mask. She recognizes the source of his power, just like his father had at the end of the opening sequence when Michael was just a child: to disarm him, she must reveal him. I gasped when I first saw the horrified expression on his face after the mask was removed. Michael is ugly and confused in that moment, blinking in the sudden light, all the threat he'd previously posed dissolving instantly in his sudden nakedness. He immediately releases Laurie in the effort to conceal himself once again, fumbling desperately with the cheap plastic. And I remember violently hating the look of him without the mask when I saw the film for the first time. My body seized with an urgent, almost unbearable need for him to put it back on.

Meanwhile, Dr. Loomis has entered the house and ascended the stairs after hearing the screams of the children whom Laurie had sent down the street to solicit the help of a neighbor. Just as Michael pauses to slip the mask back onto his face, Loomis shoots him several times in the chest. Michael recoils with each shot, stumbling and staggering backward, then falling through a window that Laurie had opened to mislead him during the earlier chase before hiding in the closet, where he attacked her. Michael lands on his back in the yard among the fallen leaves, his arms and legs splayed out to the side. The mask is still firmly in place, a gleaming white as it catches the light.

But I couldn't stop thinking about what he had looked like without it. I didn't ever want to see him like that again.

~

The days at the resort felt shorter and shorter as the morning approached when we would have to check out and begin the long drive home. I wanted to gather each moment in the sun like a postcard I could keep forever. I would stare at the older boys in the pool and try to commit their bodies to memory—bare skin bronzed by the sun, teeth dazzlingly white as they showed off their easy smiles. There was a boy on staff who was tasked each afternoon with picking up stray towels and other equipment left behind by the guests, and I would sometimes walk slowly behind him on the footpath in the shade of the palm trees, keeping several paces back while recording his every move. My body would tingle with excitement when I was able to sneak glances at the muscled abdomen that he exposed each time his shirt lifted up as he reached into a tree to remove a dead branch or a plastic bag that had flown up and gotten caught in the branches. I can still see his face, the single knowing glance he once threw back in my direction when I tripped over a stone while following him too closely as he approached the snack bar carrying a cardboard box over one shoulder.

The half-smile, the almost-wink. I would recognize him anywhere.

I was swimming alone in the pool late in the afternoon on the last day of the trip while my mother and S were upstairs sleeping off the effects of morning poolside cocktails, my brother still relegated to the indoors because of his sunburn. I paddled back and forth alone in the deep end, sneaking glances at an older boy wearing dark sunglasses splayed across a plastic lounge chair, probably dozing, a towel wrapped loosely around his waist just below his navel. I noticed that the skin on his bare chest had reddened in the afternoon sun, and I found myself paddling closer toward him until I was at the edge of the pool where I could peer up at him. Suddenly he flicked up his sunglasses and squinted in my direction, glancing over his shoulder as he tried to figure out what I was looking at. I disappeared under the water, holding my breath for as long as I could before surfacing in a different area of the pool, careful not to glance in his direction again.

Later I was doing handstands in the shallow end, seeing how long I could hold my body upright before I crashed back down into the water. When I came up and wiped my eyes, a man was standing beside me in the pool, his large hands lightly skimming the surface. He must have waded toward me from the ladder while I was still underwater. He must have stood there patiently waiting for me to come back up for air.

I hadn't noticed him before, but I realized he must have been watching me the whole time when he told me in a quiet but deep voice that I looked lonely, like I could use some company. "A boy like you should have lots of friends," he said slowly, each word heavy like the humidity in the air around us.

The man's chest was thick, and his arms looked strong. He had large white teeth that revealed themselves when he smiled patiently down from where he towered high above me in the pool, his hands still skimming the gently rippling surface as his body cast a shadow that blocked out the sun. I could see myself in the lenses of his black sunglasses, my head only barely cresting the surface of the water like the bob of a fishing lure waiting to be pulled under.

I shivered involuntarily and swiped wet hair from my forehead. I took a step backward toward the deep end, and then another.

"Do you want to play a game with me?" the man asked, speaking more quickly when he noticed my slow retreat.

A group of younger kids splashed around nearby with floatie toys and an inflatable ball, their parents lounging peacefully close at hand on pool chairs with their eyes closed and their faces turned to the sun. But no one else was swimming on our side of the pool. I was the only one who could hear what the man was saying. Someone who glanced our way might have even thought we were father and son. I didn't remember having seen this man before during the week of our stay, but that didn't mean I hadn't passed him several times on my way to and from our suite on my walks along the pathways, charting my route like an explorer, mapping a distant and dazzling land. The resort was crowded, after all. There were so many other people to look at.

He hadn't told me his name, nor did he ever ask for mine. "What kind of game?" I asked after only a brief hesitation. I'd been alone all afternoon.

"I'll show you," he said, and he widened his stance in the water, spreading his feet so that he was standing with his legs wide apart, almost like some kind of cheerleading pose. He gestured down beneath him under the water. He wore navy shorts loose at the waist, the string untied and floating up toward the surface. There was gray in the otherwise dark and coiled hairs lining his torso. He had a deep tan like the old woman who sold mango slices from a cart at the entrance to the resort, her skin like cured leather.

I learned quickly that the rules of the game were that I would swim between his legs, straddled wide at first, with the goal of not touching him at all as I swam through. Then he would narrow his stance, closing the gap between his legs and making it more and more difficult for me to pass through without our skin touching underwater. I hesitated only the first time I dove under, my hands pressed to the rough floor of the pool as I carefully maneuvered myself between his legs. I was proud of my accuracy in the first few rounds as I became more confident in my ability to swim quickly through the obstacle he'd made of his body, and I thought I was winning the game because I kept angling myself just so, bursting up above the water behind him to receive the accolades I thought I was due. The man would applaud dutifully each time before reminding me I hadn't won the game yet.

"Let's try again," he said, something new in his voice that hadn't been there before. And when I dove down once more, my eyes adjusting to the sharp sting of the chlorine in the water before I made my attempt to pass through his legs again—now much closer together than they'd been before, almost as if he was just standing there and no longer even playing the game—I saw that he had pulled himself out of his swimming shorts in the time it had taken me to go under. His cock was now lolling in the water above me, already thick and swollen.

He stepped toward me and blocked the sun again, everything going dark. I knew even back then that he had wanted me to touch him when he revealed himself to me. It was clear what this man wanted to provide for me and what I would be expected to give him in exchange, even if I didn't yet have the language for how it might have gone. And I wondered later, after the fear and confusion and disgust with myself had dulled to a gnawing sense of dread, what exactly I'd done to show him I might have wanted it. He might have seen me watching the older boys in the pool whose bodies were already lined with smooth, curved muscles snaking down their arms and torsos, loose swim shorts hanging just below the stark tan lines at their waists. He might have seen my eyes go wide when I saw how tightly their shorts clung to their midsections as they pulled themselves up the ladder out of the pool before they could adjust themselves and hide what I'd already seen outlined against the wet fabric.

Now my hands clawed toward the surface of the water above me as I imagined the man closing in on me and holding me under, his grip tight around my neck. I forced myself to look away from what he'd shown me and orient myself before it was too late. I imagined he was trying to trap me. He would never let me resurface after he saw me scrambling to escape, because then he thought I'd tell everyone what he'd done to me. He would have to drown me to keep himself safe.

Suddenly I couldn't tell which way was up or down. I splashed around in a panic, scraping my knees painfully along the bottom of the pool and pulling more and more water into my lungs as I cast about for any sense of where I was in the water. Then I finally burst up above the surface just a few feet away from where the man still stood, his hands invisible under the water now as I coughed and choked and tried to catch my breath. He slowly crossed his arms over his broad chest as he kept his eyes trained on me, and I saw myself in his sunglasses again. I was the only child left in the pool, and I looked so alone surrounded by all that blue, the surface of the water darkening behind me as it got deeper and deeper toward the diving board.

I couldn't look at him again after I'd forced myself to resurface. Something in my face would make plain what had happened. Everyone at the pool would see. Instead, I turned away from him and swam quickly toward the metal ladder to pull myself up and out of the water.

I didn't stop to gather my things—the white bath towel I'd brought down from the suite, the pair of cheap goggles too tight around my face that always left circles around my eyes when I pulled them off. I walked quickly back toward the steps leading up to our suite where I'd be able to lock myself behind a closed door and slowly calm the trembling that was already overtaking my body, my stomach in knots and my face red not only from the sun but also from what I imagined everyone who might've seen me beneath the water would now know about me.

I turned back only once, just as my hand gripped the hot metal railing next to the steps. And that's when I saw that the man from the pool was following me.

A terror seized me like nothing I'd ever felt before as I realized he was never going to let me go. He would always be there just a few steps behind me, my own bogeyman stalking me in the clear light of day. And when he finally caught me, everyone would know what I'd done. He didn't run as he pursued me either. He didn't look as if he was worried I would get away. I saw when I looked back that he had already climbed up the ladder out of the water, and he adjusted himself in his wet shorts while he rounded the bend toward the steps where I stood frozen at the sight of his approach, leaving a trail of dripping water behind him marking his path toward me across the hot concrete.

I knew I had to run. I knew he was coming for me. I scampered up the steps and turned the corner leading to the row of suites, my bare feet padding heavily down the corridor. And then I was at our door, my fists pounding frantically and vigorously just below the bronze knocker to wake up my mother and S, or to alert my brother that I was in danger.

"Open up," I said, aiming my voice through the living room window facing the courtyard, where my brother had been watching TV earlier. He should have been able to hear me even though the window was closed with the air conditioning on high, which S always demanded. But now the man had almost finished climbing the stairs. He knew which suite was mine. There was nowhere else to hide.

My mother finally came to the door and let me inside. "Stop the hammering already," she said, wincing and pressing her fingers to her temples before wiping her eyes with her thumbs as I pushed past her, barely able to hear anything she said over the blood pounding through my skull. Only a few seconds after she closed the door came a knock, quiet and polite, like someone delivering mail or dutifully returning something he had borrowed.

I stood there shivering and dripping water onto the tiled floor of the small living room while my mother went to the door again after casting a questioning glance in my direction. I couldn't find any words to say, nothing to warn her about what might happen next. When she opened it, there stood the man from the pool. He wore a polite smile that looked like something he had rehearsed in a mirror. I still couldn't see his eyes past his sunglasses as he leaned on one arm against the doorframe and crossed one ankle over the other, a towel slung casually over his shoulder that he must have grabbed from a stack as he followed me upstairs. Now it was my mother who was reflected in his lenses.

"There you are," he said, and I knew he was looking past her to where I was standing. He didn't care that she was there at all.

The man asked my mother whether I wanted to come back down and continue the game we had started, and I remember shaking my head vigorously, refusing to even look up at him from where I'd burrowed into the cushion of a cheap armchair. I focused my attention on a painting above the table in the kitchen, tropical fruit dangling from a tree branch. The cushion of the chair was completely soaked with water from the pool.

"I'm sorry," I heard my mother say to the man at the door. "I don't think he wants to play. Maybe some other time."

The man from the pool had probably come up to be sure I wouldn't tell anyone what had happened. But when he saw me, too afraid to even meet his eyes, I'm sure he knew I'd keep the secret of what had taken place between us. He had revealed nothing to me about myself that I didn't already know, except for the fact that I wasn't the only one who could tell. What I'd thought was only a secret desire had been visible on my body all along to those who knew how to look.

He had been watching me in the crowded hot tub. He'd seen me following the pool boy. I had never actually been wearing a mask at all.

~

We spent our last night in Florida at a restaurant where the booths were all crammed into the frames of antique cars, all six of us pressed tightly together between the two doors of an old Ford Thunderbird painted a gleaming red. After dinner my mother and S went for drinks at a bar overlooking the empty beach to celebrate our vacation, but I pretended to feel too sick after dinner to join the older boys at the arcade on the boardwalk, walking myself quickly back up to the suite with my brother. I sat in the dark that night on the foldout mattress in the living room of our suite, staring out the window from the edge of the couch as parents and children headed down to the pool for a late swim before closing time, groups of girls in bikini tops and denim shorts giggling with each other as their flip-flops slapped the concrete.

We checked out of the resort early the next morning. I stood next to my mother as we waited in line at the reception desk to turn in the key cards, my eyes casting about anxiously to see who might be watching. But the man from the pool wasn't lurking in the lobby behind the potted palm trees, and he wasn't hiding behind a car in the parking lot as we loaded the van and began the long drive home.

I looked out the window when we turned the corner and headed north, the resort disappearing behind the surf shops and the food trucks. I was sure I couldn't get away that easily. In a horror movie, I'd be struck down by my attacker the moment I believed I was safe, so I knew I could never let my guard down. But no one stopped us as we finally turned onto the highway ramp, S pressing down hard on the accelerator. I could no longer see the ocean.

I'd been awake all night beside my sleeping brother, listening for anyone who might be lurking outside the door, maybe even trying to somehow get inside when he thought everyone was asleep. Heavy breathing on the other side of the window, a hand pressing against the glass, leaving a mark that I'd see the next morning to let me know he'd been there watching me. And I was still listening when the snack bar opened for breakfast and the first swimmers dove into the water. All I could see when I closed my eyes was the man from the pool, even there in the back seat of the van the next morning, with S adjusting the radio dial in search of a classic rock station, my mother complaining that he needed to keep his eyes on the road.

I measured the growing distance between the resort and myself by every town and highway exit we put behind us, every gas station and fast-food drive-through window. As the sun went down, we stopped for dinner at a pizza place in Georgia where I sullenly picked at a slice while avoiding eye contact with my mother, worried what my face would give away if she looked too closely. Then we drove on through the night, the road ahead mostly empty, the occasional headlights of cars on the other side of the highway lighting up the dark like beacons from a search party scouring the night for some lost thing.

When it was my mother's turn to drive, she listened to an audiobook about a woman on the run from a house where she has witnessed a series of terrible murders. The voice of the reader finally lulled me to sleep as she described the novel's protagonist racing from her pursuer through the dark alleyways of some desolate city as he somehow got closer and closer, always closer than she imagined it was possible for him to be. I was asleep before she ever faced him. I never learned how the story ended.

11

A HEAVY, GRAY SKY HUNG LOW over the familiar landscape of our suburban Missouri county when we finally arrived back home late the next morning after the long drive through the night. As we turned onto the drive leading down the hill in our neighborhood, all the vibrant colors I'd remembered seeing from my bedroom window before the trip—the bright red of a neighbor's mailbox, orange columns on the front porch of a house across the pond, blue and purple wildflowers that had sprung up near the dock at the edge of the water—now seemed faded and dulled, barely catching my eye. No signs of life in any of the windows, everything quiet and still.

I'd never been away from home for so long, and I'd found myself worrying on the drive back that everything would be different upon our return. There could be rubble from another tornado or a massive crater where a meteor had violently struck down from outer space. But what happened was somehow worse, even more irrevocable. The neighborhood seemed impossibly bland and nondescript compared to everything I'd just seen elsewhere—the tropical gardens of the beach houses near the resort and the impossible colors of the sky over the ocean at sunrise. I wondered why anyone wanted to live here. The light from those long days at the beach didn't reach this far north, and as we had exited the highway and driven past the shabby strip malls and chain restaurants and the crowded Walmart parking lot at the central intersection before the turnoff toward the high school, I had finally seen my town for what it really was, and the shame of it sliced through any relief I'd felt about coming home.

This was no Haddonfield. There was no danger lying in wait around these bland suburban corners with overgrown weeds crowding the sewer drains, garbage cans lying on their sides at the end of a neighbor's driveway. No promise of anything sinister or surprising lurking in the shadows to emerge only when darkness fell. Michael Myers wouldn't have wasted his time. I was the only secret there that needed keeping.

And then the sight of our own house, smaller and drabber than I'd remembered it as we turned into the driveway and my mother pressed the button to open the garage door, sighing deeply as she unbuckled her seatbelt. The wooden bench on the front porch was cheap and discolored. The newly planted tree in the yard had yet to sprout any leaves, and we didn't know what to do about the bare patches in the lawn. As the garage door rolled slowly open, I looked up at my little window, where I'd spent so much time looking out at the neighborhood, and I was disgusted with myself for ever wondering whether there had been anything or anyone waiting out there for my face to appear. Someone who could have been tracking me over time, yearning to make his presence known.

No one had ever been watching at all. Now I was more alone than ever.

～

My body was stiff and cramped as I stretched my arms and legs after stepping out of the car in the garage, as if I'd somehow grown bigger while we were away and my skin had yet to stretch itself out to make room for what I had become. I knew something had changed in me, a new kind of pain searing my insides from some secret place—a shame I didn't yet know how to carry. I also realized when I got upstairs to my bedroom and looked at myself in the small mirror hanging by my closet door that I'd gotten a sunburn that last day at the pool, dead skin flaking off my neck and shoulders when I cautiously picked at the parts that hurt the most.

I looked away quickly when I caught my own gaze in the reflection.

My mother called my name from down the hall just an hour or so after we arrived home, having dropped off the van and picked up our own car from S's house, where we'd left it parked in his driveway during the trip. Ever since we got home I'd been lying on my bed and staring up at the ceiling, the thin curtain drawn over the single window. I'd run from the garage, through the house and up the stairs, and slammed my bedroom door, leaving my mother and brother to drag in the suitcases even as I heard my mother yelling for me from downstairs, her voice muffled as I dove under the covers.

That Sunday morning I couldn't imagine going back to summer camp the next day as if nothing had happened. Everyone would see that I'd been marked and forever changed, something in my face that the man in the pool had easily recognized. The other boys would sneer at me in the changing room when I slipped into my swim shorts, all of them pointing in my direction when they saw what was wrong with me. Maybe wondering how they'd never noticed before.

"I'll be right there," I called out with a groan as my mother said my name again from her bedroom, more sternly this time, like I'd be in trouble if I didn't hurry. I unlocked the door and stepped into the hall-way at the top of the stairs. My mother's bedroom was at the other end, and I could already see her unzipping my suitcase, sifting through the hastily packed contents and trying to figure out which items were clean and which needed to be added to the laundry pile.

"Can you please help me with this?" she said. She was wearing a cheap sundress that she'd bought in Florida at one of the shops on the boardwalk, the petals of a giant yellow flower exploding across her body.

She disappeared around the corner toward her closet, and I took a few steps down the hallway past the doorway to my brother's bedroom where he was kneeling on the carpet, shoving socks into the bottom drawer of his dresser, still clutching the stuffed white bear in his free hand that he'd insisted join us on the trip. He'd complained about his sunburn the whole drive home, crying out every time the van lurched into a pothole and the jolt shoved him backward in his seat. The bub-bles on his shoulders had only barely begun to heal. I'd held my hands to my ears to drown him out while he whined and complained. Now he glanced up as I passed by almost as if he had something to say to me, but I looked away and kept walking.

My mother crossed the room again just as I entered, carrying a makeup bag toward her vanity table. She carefully placed tubes of lipstick back into the drawer, neatly lining up mascara and powder next to the mirror where I'd sat staring at my own face for what felt like hours when she was making dinner or working in the yard, looking for something dark and twisted inside myself that I imagined would become visible if I took the time to look.

Now I opened the suitcase and looked down at my wrinkled clothes. The black cotton pants I'd brought for the night we went to a nice restaurant overlooking the beach that I never actually wore, my mother having needlessly worried about the possibility of a dress code. The T-shirt with the summer camp's logo stenciled onto the chest pocket. The swim shorts I'd worn on our last day in Florida, probably still wet from the pool.

"You know," said my mother from where she was standing behind me.

I looked back at her when I heard the hesitation in her voice, our eyes meeting from across the room. She pulled the stool toward her from beneath the vanity table and then sank into it with a sigh.

"You've been so quiet lately," she said finally. "You haven't been letting me in. Is there something on your mind? Did you have a good time on vacation? And I wanted to ask you about that man—"

"I'm just tired," I interrupted, turning away from her and staring at the wall as blood rushed to my face.

There was no way she could have known what had happened with the man in the pool. After all, I'd been alone the whole time. No one had been there with me. Not even the other strangers sunbathing nearby, none of them knowing what was happening underwater. And when he came to the door he said barely anything before she turned him away. But I sensed suspicion in my mother's voice even though it was likely only concern, the two always having seemed the same to me back then, as if everyone was trying to get at the root of what was wrong with me, even as I knew they'd recoil when they found out the truth.

The phone on the bedside table suddenly rang and startled my mother out of our conversation. She dropped a small jewelry box, silver chains and earrings scattering on the dark green carpet. I was so relieved when she stood up to answer the call that my hands were trembling as I lifted my crumpled T-shirts and shorts from the suitcase to take them downstairs to the laundry room. She hadn't seen my secret, and I had to get away before she did. But I was almost out the door again when I looked back at my mother, and what I saw in her face as she listened to the caller stopped me cold.

She hadn't said a word since she'd distractedly greeted the caller when she first picked up the receiver, and she was now sitting stiffly on the edge of her mattress, the spiral phone cord limp on her lap. She locked eyes with me across the room, and somehow I already knew what she was going to tell me. Or maybe it only seemed like that later when I remembered the scene, like something in a film rather than something I'd lived through, the climactic moment when everyone gets the news that changes everything forever.

My mother says my name quietly and then tells me to get my brother. I take a step back, dropping my dirty clothes to the floor. A quietly emotional music score begins to play while my mother delivers the news to my brother and me—the two of us kneeling beside her on the bed—that our father is gone. That he had died while we were in Florida. We crumple into her arms as her mouth forms words that are drowned out by the notes being struck on an invisible piano, everything going soft and murky at the edges. My brother sobs into her chest while I carefully remove my glasses before the shocked tears begin to fall down my cheeks. My mother is still holding the phone in her left hand like an anchor, and she doesn't cry as she consoles us—doesn't react to the news in any visible way at first. Then she finally drops the phone with one loud sob, and for the first time I can hear a voice coming from the receiver, someone asking if we're still there. Now the image begins to blur into a slow dissolve, the camera sweeping away.

The last time I'd used that phone was when I'd hung up on my father just before we left on our trip, when he had called while I was packing my suitcase and asked to speak to me. Our final conversation. He was already slurring his words when he asked me how I'd been lately, what I had been up to and whether I was looking forward to the vacation. He didn't mention our previous trip to Florida, and I wondered if he even remembered it. I angrily accused him of being drunk yet again, and I hung up the phone without saying goodbye. I didn't want to speak to him like that anymore. I knew by twelve years of age that not everyone's father was what he was.

But I remembered the phone call after my mother told me he was gone. I remembered what I'd said to him.

After Lynda is confronted by Michael Myers wearing the bedsheet in his half-hearted disguise, she grows frustrated by his silence as he simply stands there pretending to be Bob, pretending to be a ghost, seemingly ignoring everything she has to say. "This is going nowhere," she complains after standing up from the bed and dialing the house across the street in an attempt to reach Laurie and ask her about Annie's whereabouts, turning her back to Michael as he drops the sheet to the floor and begins to walk slowly toward her.

Laurie picks up the call right when Michael grabs Lynda from behind and begins to choke her with the telephone cord, and she hears Lynda's moans, her muffled cries for help. But after a brief hesitation, she assumes the caller to be Annie playing a joke on her. She listens to Lynda's final breaths without understanding what she's hearing, and only when the call abruptly ends without the muffled voice ever being identified does Laurie finally begin to worry. She looks out across the street just as the lights in the Wallace house go out, and no one answers when she tries to call back. That was the last time she would hear her friend alive.

I cried tears of shame when I heard the news of my father's death, and I played back our last phone conversation, remembering how poorly I had behaved toward him. I hadn't understood. I'd judged him too harshly, not even given him a chance to speak. He hadn't really been drunk at the time of the call, just so incredibly sick that his voice had changed somehow. The cancer must have returned. He had needed help and I had turned my back on him. That's what he'd been trying to tell me when he called, but I wouldn't listen. He was on many different medications at the time. I knew there were side effects. Why hadn't I given him a chance to explain? I didn't know how I could have been so cruel, and I would never get the chance to atone for what I'd done.

For years this was the story I told myself.

I wore black pants and a white shirt to my father's memorial service the following week, the same outfit I'd taken to Florida in case I needed to dress formally to eat at the nice restaurant by the beach. My mother snapped the top button of my shirt before clipping on a thin black tie she'd picked up at a department store at the mall, then stepping back to see how I looked. The fabric was tight around my neck, too tight, like I was slowly being choked to death.

"You're so grown up," she said.

My brother tugged at my arm nervously as we approached the entrance to the funeral home from the car, the sun already hot on our faces. The building was painted a bright white, the image of a cross etched carefully into the wide-open front door. I knew my brother was afraid to go inside. He was afraid to see our father. But my mother had told me that the casket would be closed for the duration of the service, and when we stepped inside, I looked down past the rows of black folding chairs facing the front of the room and saw the wooden casket resting on a podium surrounded by bouquets of flowers.

I imagined the lid flying open and my father's body bolting upright as he roared with laughter, telling us it had all been a joke. I wished he'd come back even for a moment just so that I could explain myself and apologize for what I'd said to him over the phone. But a wish like that was the wish of a child, and I wasn't a child anymore.

I sat down with my brother in the second row of chairs as the hushed voices of family and friends filled the air, some of the adults averting their eyes when they saw us. "Those poor boys," someone said. No one else was sitting down, just milling about near the front of the room, so I felt as if we were on a stage, everyone waiting to see what we would do.

My grandmother—my father's mother—had come over to our house the day after we returned from Florida, her eyes rimmed red from crying. But she smiled when she saw us, swooping us up in her arms. She took us outside to the porch while my mother tended to some chores that she hadn't yet had time for, and we watched birds skimming the surface of the small pond in the middle of the neighborhood, a few children walking along the edge of the water with a plastic bucket. She wanted to talk about our father, but I didn't know what to say. I didn't know how to explain.

Now at the funeral home I couldn't help feeling all those sad eyes studying me. I knew I should have been sobbing into my mother's dress. I knew I should have been standing at the double doors and allowing everyone to touch my shoulder as they passed by, flowers and condolence cards bursting from their arms as they told me how sorry they were about what had happened. But I felt restless, even seated up front away from the small crowd gathered at the periphery, as if I needed to run away and never stop moving—just keep running into the distance until no one could see me at all.

My brother was staring down at the stiff dress shoes that our grandmother had brought to our house the day before, after calling my mother to ask for our latest size. My own toes pressed too hard against the front of the fake leather slip-ons. "Are any of our friends coming?" he asked.

"What friends?" I said.

"From school. From camp. Does anyone know?"

"I didn't tell anyone."

My brother sighed sadly, fidgeting with the buttons lining the front of his shirt. I'd never seen him wear clothes like that before, and he seemed so strange to me in that moment, like someone else's brother. I didn't recognize him.

"I can't breathe in here," I said.

My brother just kept his head down, trying not to look up at the casket. Probably trying not to imagine our father's body inside it.

After a while I stood up and managed to push quietly past a refreshments table and escape into the lobby. My mother caught my eye from a corner where she was talking to some of her old friends from high school who had brought pictures of my father as a teenager for the collage assembled on poster board near the guest book. A hundred versions of my father's younger face smiled out at me, and I squirmed when I noticed our shared features for the first time, looking away when I thought for a second that a picture of him as a child had been of me instead. There was a photograph of him holding me as a baby, another where he was holding my hand as we walked down a gravel driveway in the woods. Finally, a picture taken during the visit to the pumpkin patch, the witch cackling behind us as my father guides me away.

I slipped through a door in the lobby into a hallway leading back toward the main office and a series of closed doors. I leaned my back against the wall and slid slowly to the floor. The hallway was empty, the walls white and antiseptic like a hospital. The fluorescent lights were almost blinding, but I didn't intend to leave until I was dragged away by my mother. Then the door opened and a girl around my age stood there, looking at me with a curious expression on her face, as if I was an exhibit in a museum and she'd already come too close. She must have followed me from the lobby, but I hadn't seen her there. For a moment I wondered if she was a ghost, but I knew better. She was thin with straight white hair and a solemn face, in a white dress with one loose strap over each shoulder. Then I suddenly recognized her from pictures of the side of my father's family I'd never met.

"I'm your cousin," she said, confirming what I'd just realized. Now I knew why she was there.

I stared unblinking at her pale cheeks, slightly flushed, and remembered the stories I'd heard about her from my father and my grandparents. How she was prone to fits of violence, then weeks when she wouldn't speak at all. How she'd been kicked out of school for attacking the other children. I was suddenly afraid of her. I didn't want her there with me. I didn't know what she would do, just the two of us there in the empty hallway.

"Thanks for coming," I said weakly. My voice echoed off the walls. She nodded and closed the door gently behind her. "Can I join you?" she asked. And when I didn't say anything in response, she lowered herself to the tiled floor and we sat together cross-legged with our knees almost touching, the fluorescent light flickering above us. The voices from the room where my father was lying in his casket were muffled and far away, the chatter like a low rumble from deep within the earth.

"We're in a spaceship," said my cousin, her eyes lighting up as she watched me with her head slightly bowed.

"What?" I asked. I was still frightened of her, my senses on high alert.

"Imagine we're in a spaceship," she said. "We've been floating in space for years. Our home planet is so far away."

I smiled then, already feeling more at ease. "A spaceship," I said. I made a beeping sound with my voice, calling up an imaginary microphone. "Houston, we have a problem."

She laughed. "Let's explore the ship," she said.

My cousin jumped to her feet and offered me her hand, her eyes meeting mine again. We walked farther down the hallway. The first door she tried to open was locked, but she just shrugged and continued on. I knocked on the door as I passed by. "Anybody home?" I asked. Then a chill went through me as I realized the room might hold someone like my father, someone else waiting to be put on display before burial.

When my cousin turned the handle on the second door, there was a creak in the hinge as it swung open, and my heart began thudding in my chest at the prospect of what we might find inside. She groped in the dark for a light switch, and I followed her as she moved farther into the room, deeper into the shadows. "I can't find anything," she said.

I began walking in the opposite direction, running my hand lightly along the wall as I moved farther and farther from the open door. The sense of not knowing what was in the room with us was almost too much to bear.

"Nothing?" I said, just as I was jabbed sharply in the gut by some large heavy thing looming in the darkness. I cursed under my breath as I heard the click of a string being pulled, an overhead light suddenly coming to life. And then I saw the coffins.

The room was lined with coffins of every color and style, more than twenty of them stuffed into the cramped windowless space. My breath caught in my throat at the sight of them, and I stumbled back hard against the wall. But then I looked at the strange girl across the room and saw that she was doubled over with laughter, her hand pressed to her mouth to keep the guffaws from spilling out. I realized my face must have been a mask of horror, drained of color, my eyes bulging cartoonishly wide. How silly everything suddenly seemed. And I caught her laughter like a sickness, both of us now on the floor and looking across at each other beneath the metal stands holding up the coffins, almost as if we were the ones waiting to be buried.

I suddenly remembered the other story about my cousin—the story of what happened to her that must have made her the way she was. The terrible thing she'd seen. She had been only six years old when she discovered her father's body in the bathroom of her house, dangling from a rope. My own father had told me the story when he thought I was old enough to hear. I imagined my cousin screaming when she saw her father, what he'd done to himself, never expecting him to be there when she opened the door. She would have been able to tell from his eyes that he was already gone—or maybe she'd been confused, wondered how he'd gotten himself into such a strange position. Maybe she'd asked him to stop, told him to get down from there. He was scaring her.

"The land of the dead," she eventually managed to say through her laughter as I wondered whether I'd also be marked now by what had happened to my father, whether my cousin and I would now be the same. "We're in the underworld!"

When she got to her feet, she started flipping the lights on and off by clicking the switch on a nearby wall—on and off, on and off, the coffins disappearing and then popping back into view. "They're alive!" she said, and suddenly I imagined the possibility that the room wasn't just a storage location for unused caskets, but rather that each one held a body, and they were all going to come alive and chase us out of the room, all the way back to the light. Maybe we were in a zombie movie now. The whole world wanted to eat us, chomp down hard on our flesh with rotten teeth and rip us open so that everyone could see what was inside of us. We were the last ones not to have been transformed into beasts, and now we had to save ourselves from certain doom.

We ran back out into the hallway, laughing and pretending to scream in horror. And when we flung open the first door we'd come through from the lobby, falling breathlessly to our hands and knees onto the carpeted floor outside the empty hallway, I saw that the lounge area at the front of the funeral home was no longer empty as it had been before. Everyone had spilled out from the viewing room with their plastic cups and small paper plates, many of them already quietly gathering their things while my brother wailed in the middle of the room, my mother smoothing his hair and trying to comfort him.

Everyone turned at once to look at us as we stumbled out. The fatherless children, our faces slowly being drained of the unbecoming glee we'd conjured up on this saddest of days.

"I told you not to leave his side," said my mother, tears glinting at the corners of her own eyes. "You scared him half to death. He thought you were gone. He was all by himself in there."

I finally took my brother's hand to help my mother calm him down, whispering half-hearted apologies as he sniffed and blew his nose into a napkin my mother held in her hands. I looked around the room for my cousin, wondering where she'd gone. I finally saw her in a corner by an empty coat rack being scolded by her own mother for what she'd done—what we'd done together. And she waved at me with a backward glance as her mother pulled her away and out the door of the funeral home into the blazing hot sun that beat down on the pavement of the parking lot, a whoosh of heat spilling into the room before her mother slammed it shut behind her.

I never saw her again.

~

I returned to summer camp with my brother one week after our father's funeral, two weeks since we'd last been there, before the trip to Florida.

Not much time had passed, but I knew I wasn't the same boy anymore. I felt like I had a different body, one with new powers that I didn't know if I'd ever be able to control.

I walked toward the camp pavilion that first morning before the announcements came over the loudspeaker, and it was as if my senses had all been heightened, the volume of the world all turned up. My muscles roiled beneath my skin like underground creatures waking up from a long sleep, hungry and ferocious. My brother and I didn't tell any of the other campers about our father's death, and I had told no one at all about the man from the pool at the resort. The only thing anyone knew was that we'd gone to Florida. I had the suntan to prove it, as well as the seashells I'd managed to bring back intact after scouring the beach for them during those first few days, wrapping them carefully in tissue paper and hiding them between the dirty clothes in my suitcase for the long drive home.

My brother's sunburn had mostly healed by then, the new skin raw and pink on his shoulders where the bubbles had been. But everyone at the pool still pointed at him on that first day back, and he hid in the bathroom stall for the rest of the swimming period.

Everyone could tell something in me had changed. I was angry and violent. I fought with the other boys, most of them younger than me, every perceived slight taking on an exaggerated magnitude in my mind. I tossed one boy from the top of the slide on the playground down onto the gravel below, blood from a gash on his arm coloring the rocks as he wailed in pain. I tripped another boy as he raced past me at second base during a kickball game and watched him tumble to his knees, his face hitting the ground hard and coming up muddy and swollen. And I yelled at the counselors when they tried to calm me down, even the counselor I'd loved before he betrayed me. Especially the counselor I'd loved.

I fought back in a mindless rage when other hands were placed on my body. I was a fast runner, and I would madly sprint away from the counselors and the other campers into the woods, blood pounding in my skull and a scream always bubbling up in my chest and clawing its way into my throat like something toxic I'd swallowed that had now become a part of me forever. The branches of the trees I scrambled past cut into my arms and legs as I ran, but I didn't care. I wanted it to hurt.

Thin streams of blood from the open wounds slicked down my exposed skin as I pounded on the fences of the houses bordering the camp where I'd once sat so peacefully on those long afternoons alone, kicking the mesh until the fence bent inward at jagged angles and pulling at planks with my bare hands until the nails came loose, my fingers raw from the effort.

Someone must have eventually called the camp's main office to complain about me, someone who lived in one of the houses. Someone had been watching after all. I wasn't surprised when I heard my name over the loudspeaker one morning as I was called to the director's office for another meeting. Maybe I'd even been expecting it—waiting for it. And when I sat down in the seat where I'd once been told to stop following the counselor with the beautiful smile, a day that now seemed ages ago, I squinted hard at the director from the other side of her desk.

"I know what's going on," she began.

My mouth fell open as I leaned back against the chair, the metal spokes digging into my shoulders. "What do you mean?" I said. I spat the words at her, my tone sharp and cold. I felt my face burn as it always did when I thought someone could see to the core of me, the rotten parts I tried to keep hidden there. But the camp director just rubbed her hands on the thighs of her khaki shorts and then clasped them together over a pile of papers on her desk.

"I'm so sorry for your loss," she said, as if she thought she knew everything about what was happening to me. I could have laughed in her face, how ridiculous she looked to me right then. And I allowed myself a whoosh of breath, my body slumping down again as I looked away from her strained gaze. She had only meant that she knew about my father. Of course.

"I know it's only natural to act out in these circumstances—"

"I'm not acting out," I said. I dug the toe of my sneaker along the cracks in the dirty floor below the chair, making a long smear in the grime.

"—but we can't keep after you like this," she continued. "We need to be a team here."

I sneered. "What are you saying?"

"You'll be all grown up soon," she said. "You need to set a good example for the other boys. You need to behave."

I bolted suddenly to my feet. The director looked startled and rolled backward in her chair, just enough for me to know I'd scared her. Then I balled my hands into fists.

"Leave me alone," I said slowly, drawing out the words and adding a threat beneath them, some promise of what I might do next. "You can't do anything to me."

"Think about what I'm saying to you," she called after me as I ran from the pavilion toward the woods, but I wasn't going to listen to her anymore. I didn't care about anything she could possibly say to me. I held my hands to my ears and screamed and screamed to drown her out.

I was removed from camp long before the end of summer, when I would have reached the upper age limit for attendance. Long before school was scheduled to start again. And my mother decided that it wasn't worth driving only my brother each day to camp and paying the expensive fee while I lingered at home alone and could have been watching him instead. She sat me down at the kitchen table one morning, both hands clutching a large coffee mug as she leaned against the kitchen counter, still wearing her robe, exhaustion plain on her face.

"Things have to be different now," she said, and I almost laughed at her just as I'd wanted to laugh at the camp director for how little she really knew about what was happening inside of me. Then she continued, "I need you to keep him safe when I'm not here. You'll be a man soon."

Now my brother and I would stay home during the day for the rest of the summer, all because I couldn't contain my violence around others. But what happened was that my brother became my target instead of those other boys at camp. I was impossibly cruel to him on those long days when he was in my care. Everything he did would send me into a rage.

I was annoyed by the way he followed me around in the house and outside in the yard, always wanting to be involved in whatever I was doing, whether it was bouncing on the backyard trampoline or catching frogs down at the pond, as the days grew longer and longer. I was annoyed by his easy laughter at a time when I did not laugh at all, and then I was made furious by how easily he cried when he recognized my cruelty for what it was. How fragile he seemed. How it would be so easy to break him. The smallest cut on his hands from climbing the trees behind the house would send him into a screaming fit. He also had a weak stomach, sometimes vomiting immediately after eating a meal because he'd shoveled the food down his throat too quickly. I was disgusted when I was forced to listen to him retch in the bathroom, and sometimes I would throw away the rest of my own meal, stomping upstairs and slamming the door to my bedroom as loudly as I could so he knew it was because of him that I was so angry.

One hot afternoon I finally relented after he'd been begging me to play a game with him. His friends had gone to the movies for the afternoon to escape the heat, and we were having a free-throw contest at the basketball hoop at the foot of a neighbor's driveway. The sun kept getting in my eyes each time I took a shot, and I was so frustrated by how badly I was doing that I didn't realize my brother had won the game until he was celebrating by laughing and pointing in my direction. He was probably only surprised and delighted that he'd won, but I was suddenly so enraged that I chased him back into the house, my feet slapping the hot concrete behind him like bullets that had missed their mark.

He must have seen something change in me after he jeered about his winning shot, because he had a head start as he tore through the kitchen door from the garage and raced up the stairs toward his bedroom. I cursed and pounded on the locked door so hard after he slammed it shut in my face that the wood splintered and the cheap lock snapped. When I pummeled my way into his bedroom, my body was filled with so much anger that I felt as if I'd explode if I didn't let it out. I burst in with my hands already clenched in fists, fingernails digging painfully into my palms. Perhaps this would be when my transformation would take place. I remembered my father's fist hovering inches from my face that night in the old house, the rough hands of the boy down the street pushing me to the floor. And I can still see the shocked expression on my brother's face when I came clamoring through the locked door, the sudden fear blazing up in his eyes as he realized there were no limits to what I might do to him.

He didn't know what it would take to make me stop. Maybe there was nothing anyone could do. He cowered in the far corner of the room on his twin bed with his back to the wall, tears already flowing from eyes wide with terror.

I lowered my fists and stepped slowly back into the hallway after I saw my brother's face, blinking in shock as if the lights had suddenly been thrown on in what had previously been an entirely dark room. He was crying as if I'd been a stranger trespassing in our house, someone he didn't know breaking down the walls and forcing their way inside. He was afraid for his life. And the sight of the stuffed animals propped against the wall on his bed that he desperately clung to now had instantly emptied me of fury and left behind only a hollowness at the pit of my stomach, a gnawing sense of everything I lacked. I was no brother. I was nothing at all. And before I retreated silently to my own bedroom, I saw that the hamster in the cage on his dresser was staring in my direction, almost as if it was trying to categorize me from what it knew of the animal kingdom—trying to see whether I still posed a threat.

I'd spent the childhood that I shared with my brother always trying to evade him, pushing him to the edge of my story to keep him safe from becoming ensnared by it and dragged down with me into the dark. Instead of comforting him when he was afraid or inviting him along when he wanted my company, I had only made him a shadow, something that would disappear from view completely when all the light was gone. But now he'd seen what my body could do. All the rage I'd kept to myself until then. I couldn't hide anymore.

Many years later, I would see my brother kiss another boy at his college graduation party when he thought no one was watching, the two of them glancing around the crowds of friends and classmates before allowing themselves that quick moment together. Late at night at a bar in uptown Chicago, dark and loud enough that he'd take the risk with both my mother and me there to celebrate with him. I'd only recently entrusted my mother with the truth about myself, a cautious conversation that became easier over time, but my brother had never shared with me the fact that kissing a boy was something he'd wanted to do. He hadn't ever trusted me enough to tell me.

When I saw him kissing the boy at the party, I thought about the night he'd been awake when I came back from the woods, wet leaves clinging to my dirty clothes. He asked where I'd been, and I'd lied to him so that he wouldn't ever follow me there. I had thought at the time that the darkness I'd been wandering through had been an obstacle put in place just for me. I thought I was alone there. But he'd been there, too, right next to me, neither of us seeing the other as we groped blindly toward the faintest glimmer of light. Only when we'd finally made it through could we ever tell anyone about what had happened there.

Who would tell the story of what it was like for Little Red Riding Hood inside the wolf if the hunter had never cut her out, this little girl who had been gobbled up, believing herself to be lost forever? I want to know what happened in those lonely hours before she stuffed the wolf's body full of stones, filling the space left by her escape. I want to know who guided her back to the village at the end of that long night, and what she said to her family when they welcomed her home and asked about her time in the woods. We privately map the contours of the dark forests we find ourselves in, learning through trial and error where its borders are the weakest and most permeable. And we always have to escape alone. But we can leave behind no map for those who step into the shadows after us, because every darkness tells a different story.

~

I spent the rest of the summer alone in my upstairs bedroom, locked away with the secret thoughts and desires that now screamed through my brain all day and night. Especially at night. I would be looking out the window as twilight encased the neighborhood in its soft glow, and I watched as darkness fell, lights winking on in the houses on the other side of the pond as happy families returned home to one another. Sometimes the sound of laughter drifted through the air from a nearby yard where someone was searing meat on an outdoor grill. Children shrieked as they chased each other down the street.

I would hear my mother arrive home from work each night, the garage door opening just below my bedroom and the clank of her keys tossed onto the kitchen counter as she kicked off her work shoes before making dinner. But I didn't come down for meals, not even when she begged me from the other side of my locked door. I grazed on snacks from the pantry after everyone else had gone to sleep, sneaking through the dark and quiet house to and from my room like a vagabond, like someone who did not belong there. I was Michael Myers in his padded room, the true nature of his desires concealed behind an otherwise blank stare. I became a teenager just over a month after my father's funeral. I entered adolescence at the end of a summer in which I waited up every night in darkness. I was afraid that if I succumbed to sleep then I would succumb to death. Death was everywhere that summer, all around me, my father and T and all the people in my dream. And I felt death in my own body like a steady beat sounding from deep inside, reminding me always of what I really was and what the future would hold for boys like me.

My mother had recorded various movies from cable television onto blank VHS tapes when we stayed at S's house while ours was being built, and I watched the horror films she'd copied for me over and over again on the small TV above my bed in an effort to stay awake each night and avoid the long hallway of my dreams. I became acquainted with other villains like Michael Myers, each with his own particular brand of desire—his own distinct method of seeing what he wanted most come to pass. I was giving myself an education in what to expect from the world, or at least in how I expected the world to eventually receive me. Those long nights alone in the dark were spent paralyzed at the threshold of a reckoning I couldn't yet imagine. I knew my story had finally begun that day at the pool with the man in Florida, my sense of his steady approach from somewhere behind me sending chills up my spine each time I relived the encounter alone in my room, remembering the sturdiness of his body and the confidence in his gaze as he stared me down. I just didn't know what came next, and no one was there to show me.

Sometimes in the bathroom mirror at night I'd see T's sad and ghostly face looking back at me for just a quick moment as I flipped on the lights before my eyes adjusted, and then it was just me again, my face slack with exhaustion.

The house that I think of now as my childhood home is the house where I spent that summer of my father's death. The summer of the trip to Florida. I haven't been back in many years, but I can see it online after a few clicks and scrolls, an image popping up clear as day. The tree we planted in the front yard is now the tallest one in the neighborhood, obscuring the house from the street and blocking the view from the window that had once been mine. When I imagine returning, I follow the long curve of the state road past the white clapboard walls of the funeral home where my father's memorial service was held, past the Chinese restaurant owned by the family of a girl I knew at school, past the home goods store where we'd gone to buy compost soil when my mother and I planted an apple tree in the backyard. There are new houses that hadn't been there before, stone welcome signs at the entrances to other neighborhoods leading to manicured backyards and white wooden fences abutting the road. There's even a sports bar in a dilapidated strip mall just before the low-rent apartment complex where people hang their laundry out to dry in plain view of the interstate. Then finally the sharp bend at the top of the hill toward the highway where the sight of the train tracks in the distance tells me I am almost home.

On this imagined journey, I turn into the neighborhood circle, driving slowly past the pond on my left with the fountain and small dock where children play, the children of people I wouldn't recognize if I saw them washing cars in driveways or watering their lawns with garden hoses. And then I'd see my old house, the windows dark and empty in the early evening twilight, always twilight when I imagine going back to that house—always near dark, the long night ahead always close at hand.

But now I see that the windows are not entirely empty after all. There's a familiar boy looking out at me from upstairs. Twelve years old, small and afraid. He hides behind a curtain with his palm pressed to the glass, and he doesn't welcome me inside. Maybe he recognizes me even from the distance of years, and he gestures violently for me to leave, to turn the car around and speed away as quickly as I can before anyone knows I'm there. I'm in danger if I stay there with him. He is not safe company. He doesn't know yet what is coming for him, but he suspects that it is relentless and cruel and that it will never stop until it consumes him completely.

Finally I turn away. I can't bear to look at him any longer.

12

THAT LONG SUMMER, and then the years that followed. The boy at the window watched his body and face changing as I stared down my reflection in the glass. Sometimes I would go for long runs on the back streets, past our neighborhood and into the woods and the hills north of the highway, all those winding roads, answering my body's cry for release from the cage I'd made of it. I never did try out for track and field, but that didn't mean my body wasn't desperate to run and run and maybe never stop moving until it had spent everything it had and could only then finally be at rest.

On one of these late afternoon sprints I got myself lost and completely turned around. The rush of my body slicing through the air was the only thing I was paying attention to until a heavy rain began to fall and I realized I no longer recognized my surroundings, no longer knew where I was. A panic came bubbling up in my chest as I tried to catch my breath, my head swiveling around anxiously. I saw a gravel driveway leading back to a house mostly hidden by the trees, a junked tractor in a ditch near a pile of newspapers wrapped in plastic that no one had ever claimed. Nothing familiar, nothing to tell me which way to go. I had to retrace my steps through trial and error as the storm grew fiercer and the sky darkened ominously, thunder rumbling in the distance and the trees bending over in the wind. But finally I saw a familiar street sign and then I sprinted all the way home, the road leading down toward our house unfurling before me like the long hallway in my dream.

Except now I was the only one still there. I'd already passed all the other people huddled against the wall, all those bloodied bodies littering the ground as I'd walked past. Now there was only the shadowy figure ahead of me still awaiting our inevitable confrontation. Everyone else was gone.

~

I developed smooth lines of muscle on my arms and chest from exercising in my bedroom, pushing against the weight of my body until it felt like something solid and almost strong. As dark stubble appeared across my cheekbones, a man was emerging from the frightened boy I'd been before. When I was fifteen years old and grocery shopping with my mother, she sent me back from the checkout line to grab some produce we'd forgotten. An older man not quite my mother's age caught my eye over the bins of fruits and vegetables in the brightly lit aisle near the front of the store. He had a body cultivated in a gym, muscles showcased by the tank top he wore tight against his broad chest. I liked his neatly trimmed beard and the colorful tattoo splashed across one shoulder. I liked the hint of a smile on his lips as he took me in.

I grabbed what I needed and turned to leave, but a glance over my shoulder showed me he was still looking. And I knew that someday I'd understand how to respond to him in kind, a new language lurking just below the surface of the world I'd known until then.

Another time I was walking alone through the mall, past the piercing booths and the holiday gift displays, when I saw a group of boys huddled together at a table near the outer perimeter of the food court. These boys wore fashionable clothes like the ones I'd seen in catalogs, jeans distressed at the knees and thighs, button-down shirts rolled up at the cuffs. One of them was giggling and looking my way as he whispered to his friends, each of them glancing sidelong at me as they sized me up after this boy pointed me out. He was thin and delicately beautiful, with silver studs in each ear that sparkled beneath the fluorescent lights. The blush coloring his cheeks when he met my eyes made him seem warm and kind, his body something that it would be safe to be close to. But at the time I'd been furious—the way these boys whispered and conspired, how together they had seen right through me and figured out what I was without a single word from my mouth. I didn't care that at the same time I also wanted to be swallowed up by them, to have them tell me everything they knew about how to be in the world like that. How they had found each other, how long they'd known. Maybe the blushing boy and I could go off alone together somewhere, and he could show me everything I'd been so desperate to learn.

Only later would I realize I could have just walked right up and joined them when I'd seen them notice me, taking my own seat at the table. I could have smiled widely at them instead of turning away and bolting in the other direction without even a glance over my shoulder to see if my reaction had hurt the boy who had been the one to notice me.

My mother gave me her old car on my sixteenth birthday, the teal Toyota that I would later wreck on an icy back road late at night while driving aimlessly alone, as I often did in the couple of years before moving to the city for college. I was finally able to drive the hour-long journey on the highway alone toward the bright lights of downtown St. Louis in search of the kind of place where I might meet other boys like me, ignoring the warnings I'd heard all my life about what might happen if I found myself alone on those dangerous streets after dark. I was ready to risk everything.

I'd read about a bar in an online advertisement that promised boys dancing for tips in a wonderland of bright lights and glitter and fog, and I printed out the directions and kept them folded and buried in my glove compartment until I knew the way by heart. Always nestled beside me on these drives to the bar was a bottle of vodka I'd borrowed from my mother's liquor cabinet, which I'd gulp from for courage in a parking lot around the corner before going inside each Saturday night. Alone in my car, I'd wait for the buzz to hit and something in my brain to spring to life as the alcohol raced down, burning the back of my throat until I couldn't feel it at all.

The bouncer didn't check IDs on the eighteen-and-up college night, just slapped a neon wristband on anyone under age to prevent them from ordering drinks. My head would be spinning from the vodka that I'd guzzled down in my car, and my heart was thudding with excitement as I passed beneath the rainbow flag and sparkling disco ball above the door. I took in the pulsing music and watched all those bodies from some dark corner, too afraid to speak to anyone for fear that the spell would be broken or I'd be found unworthy and made to leave. I just mumbled short replies when questioned nonchalantly by the bouncer, or when I was asked my name by a boy on the dance floor who had just thumbed glitter across my cheekbones, looking away when he winked at me or tried to press his body closer to mine. I was still too afraid to allow myself a taste of what I wanted most.

Once a much older man appeared out of nowhere with a sudden grip firm on my crotch as he leaned in close where I was perched on a bar stool surveying the crowd, a dazed and loopy smile likely gracing my young face after the vodka had done its work. He smelled of booze and sweat, and I saw something in his eyes that made me instinctively shove his hand away. He cursed me and shoved his middle finger in my face before stumbling back into the crowd, his round belly leading the way. I didn't see him again until later, when I gently pushed open a stall door in the restroom and his hands were suddenly and without warning pushing me forward into the dirty wall covered with scribbled epithets, phone numbers, crude drawings.

"I'll kill you, you little tease," he growled.

The scent of him reminded me of my father. He was already drunk, and I managed to duck under his arms and run free, my heart racing as I rushed back out through the swinging door past another wall of graffiti and a shelfful of empty cocktail glasses. I disappeared onto the dance floor, the bodies of the beautiful boys beneath the bright disco ball forming a kind of shield keeping me safe. I'd usually stay until last call, sipping the dregs of abandoned drinks when the bouncer wasn't looking, waiting until the overhead lights were finally flipped on harsh and bright before the last of us were ushered out to make the long drive home.

I always held my breath over the bridge.

My father hadn't been much older than I was at the time of the accident that mangled his arm. But maybe he was in the passenger seat beside me on those drives when I thought I was all alone, the lights in the distance doubling and tripling in size as my head swam and my eyelids drooped low from the exhaustion brought on by the booze and the dancing and the inviting darkness outside the car. The glow of the city faded in the distance behind me as the highway cut straight through the floodplains and down toward the river. Maybe my father had quietly steered me to safety, keeping watch until I made it home.

One night while driving back from the bar on yet another Saturday night, I impulsively pulled off the highway when I saw the sign for the cemetery up ahead and drove down the tree-lined pathways past the small ponds and the more ostentatious memorials until I knew from memory that I was close to my father's grave. I gulped down the few remaining shots from the vodka bottle in the car, staring hard at the darkness outside the windshield. But when I finally dragged myself out to make the search on foot, I kept getting turned around and heading the wrong way down the neatly arranged rows of headstones, sometimes almost tripping over the bouquets of flowers that had been left in the metal vases attached to the markers and once falling to my knees when I slipped on the wet grass. No one was there to see me except for maybe a groundskeeper who would have kept his distance, watching to see what I'd be getting up to alone in the cemetery long after midnight.

I tried to remember the day of the funeral so that I could orient myself that way. Was that the tree where I took cover when the sun had been too hot on my face, the sweat pooling up in the armpits of my stiff shirt while I pressed my arms tight to my sides to stop myself from trembling? Was that the bench where my grandmother sat down when the heat of the day had made her dizzy and faint? But I didn't find my father that night. I finally returned to my car and sobbed with my face pressed against the steering wheel until I was at least calm enough to drive the remaining miles home, my failure to locate his final resting place knotting itself inside of me into a new kind of shame to add to what was already there.

~

After my high school graduation, I moved into the student housing at a university downtown and continued spending my weekend nights at the bar I'd discovered when I was sixteen, but I knew even then that I needed to be further away from the boy in the window. The boy I'd been before. I could still see him at the bar, crossing that threshold for the first time, the way he held himself as if he didn't deserve any of the happiness he'd hoped to find there. I didn't want to be reminded of him anymore.

I visited New York alone on a whim during fall break with savings I'd earned working for S at his construction company over the summer, and when the semester was over, I filled up a rented car with everything I could carry for the long drive. The end of one story, the beginning of another. I rented a small bedroom from an online listing in a cheap, crowded apartment deep in an industrial neighborhood in Brooklyn I'd never known existed until I moved there, streets littered with plastic bottles and layers of graffiti smeared onto warehouse walls. It was what I could afford with the money my mother continued to send, and I was mugged on the street for the six-packs of cheap beer that I learned to hide beneath my coat for the short walk from the corner deli to the front door of my building. Beers that I'd drink warm on the cheap mattress tossed onto the floor of my back bedroom because I knew how quickly they would disappear from the shared refrigerator. The recent college graduates I lived with threw loud parties almost every night in the common spaces while I huddled next to a desk lamp on the floor with the door closed, reading the paperback books I'd brought from home— horror novels from my mother's shelves, the same books I'd read as a child—until my vision dimmed pleasantly at the edges from the beer, the world spinning gently around me.

Stories about characters running blind through the dark from whatever might be chasing them. Stories about monsters hiding in the shadows.

The boy at the window was so far away.

I'll always remember the last night I made the long drive back to my childhood home from the bar in St. Louis before I moved away for good. Winter break was over, all my things already packed up in suitcases that I'd pushed against the wall in my old bedroom. Everyone stumbled from the bar through the rainbow streamers and onto the city streets at the usual hour, last call having come and gone, only to see that a heavy fog had settled over the area since we'd gone inside. I could barely see the pavement in front of me as I took each careful step through the dark toward my car, my hands outstretched before me as if I could somehow clear a path for myself through the mist. To anyone watching, it would have looked like I was afraid of something that might be hiding there in the dark. What might be waiting just ahead of me, materializing only after it was too late to run.

I drove for almost two hours through the fog, guided through the hazy darkness only by the taillights of the car in front of me. I thought of my mother while I sat in traffic on the bridge across the river, unable to hold my breath for long before it would force itself back out. I'd never told her where I went on those long nights. She was probably asleep at home in the house by the pond while I danced beneath those colored lights, maybe imagining that I was somewhere hanging out with friends, playing board games in a basement, perhaps drinking a beer or two we'd snuck from someone's father's stash. Nothing more than that. She never knew how far from home I'd gone. Never knew how long it sometimes took for me to make it back.

I finally pulled off the highway that foggy night and drove the last mile down the state road before entering the turnoff into our neighborhood just as dawn broke in the sky above. Now, in my memory, the drive through the fog feels like a long goodbye. I was leaving just a few days later, I had mailed the security deposit for the apartment in Brooklyn, and nothing was going to keep me from driving away as fast as I could. Not even the thick air around me that I felt was trying to close in and trap me there forever. I couldn't see past the sidewalk on the service road leading toward my neighborhood, so it struck me that I could have been anywhere at all. I could have stumbled into another world when I exited the highway. I could have even driven straight onto the familiar streets of Haddonfield, the houses all waiting for me there in the dark, flickering candlelight in the windows inviting me to come closer.

Maybe I would be mistaken for Michael Myers returning home after many years away.

13

THE HOUSE BY THE POND where I'd spent those lonely teenage years was sold when my mother finally married S, after my brother went away to college in Chicago and S's company hit a good run of business. The two of them moved to a neighborhood we never could have afforded to live in when I was a child. The same town where we'd lived with our father and then afterward at the townhouse, another neighborhood that hadn't been there before.

The front of the new house is a thick wall of real brick, the porch framed by tasteful white columns. Flowers planted by the previous owners spring up each year along the footpath leading down to the driveway. The maple tree in the front yard is decades old, its branches thick with leaves in the summer months, blocking the upstairs windows from a view of the street. The backyard opens onto a golf course just past a white picket fence, and a community swimming pool and recreation center are just down the hill. My mother goes on walks at twilight along a paved path through a light smattering of trees dotting the carefully landscaped fairway behind the house, neighbors waving politely as she passes by.

I flew back from New York to help her get settled shortly after she moved in, as well as to go through my things from the old house to see what I wanted to keep and what I wanted to throw away. I was living with another man in Brooklyn by then, a home we'd made over the course of several years together. I never thought about where I'd grown up anymore, the boy I'd been when I was there. And I didn't take anything back with me in the end. I didn't want to remember.

My mother picked me up from the airport just after dusk, and we drove down the mostly empty and darkening highway toward the new house. I looked out the window when we were almost there, after we'd crossed the river, when we'd laughed out loud as we each took a deep breath just before we drove onto the bridge. I saw the shopping mall where I'd sometimes gone alone as a teenager to follow beautiful boys from store to store, yearning for them with a force so strong that I sometimes thought could make everything I touched burst into flame. The bookstore where I'd steal copies of magazines filled with pictures of male models staring right out at me from the glossy pages, too ashamed to pay for them at the register but too entranced to leave them behind. I noticed the dollar theater where my father had taken us a few times after the divorce, memories flooding back of gummy candy and fountain soda and my father beside me, ready to playfully jab my ribs during the scary parts. And then just up the road was the cemetery where he was buried, dark now and sprawling out in the distance north of the highway, but still sparking memories of that hot day in July when we'd seen him lowered into the ground.

I didn't comment on how close we were to both the old townhouse and the house we'd once shared with my father as my mother pulled off the highway and our headlights illuminated a road that was now a few lanes wider than when I was a child, freshly paved with flowers lining the sidewalks. The trees between the townhouses and on my father's street where I'd often hidden myself away had long ago been cut down to make room for even more new houses, but the gas station where I'd stolen candy as a child was still there. I could see the turnoffs to both neighborhoods as we veered instead onto another street before finally pulling into the driveway of my mother's new house. She sighed contentedly as the garage door opened.

S was still at the bowling alley bar with a few friends, and as I hauled my backpack from the trunk after we'd parked in the garage, my mother said he'd probably be home late and that we wouldn't have to wait up for him. "You know how he is when he gets together with the boys," she said as she opened the door from the garage into the kitchen, clearly excited to show me the house for the first time. I remembered how I'd spent my own time at the bowling alley back when I was a child, how I'd eagerly watched those same men from my secret hiding spot. But I quickly pushed the thought away.

My brother couldn't get time off from his new job that he'd taken after graduation, so it would be just the two of us that night. He would come for his things another time.

We ordered pizza from her favorite delivery place, and my mother told me over and over again how happy she was that I was back at home, leading me from room to room while we waited for the food to arrive and showing me the new furniture she and S had ordered, the paintings they'd bought to remember the various vacations they'd taken together. A watercolor of a Florida palm tree loomed above the fireplace mantel, a bright orange sunrise cresting over the horizon in the distance. I admired the dramatic living room windows looking out onto the golf course, the clear night sky full of stars. I noticed some of the same furniture we'd had at the old house arranged in new configurations around the many rooms, and something in me lurched at the realization that I'd never see the old house again—at least not the way it had been. The boy at the window would be trapped there forever.

My mother and I were each carrying a glass of wine from a bottle she'd immediately opened to mark the occasion. I'd already had several mini bottles of merlot on the plane and cocktails at the airport before that, and my head was swimming by the time we sat down in the cozy basement den with the open pizza box on the coffee table in front of us. A familiar fuzziness taking over.

We leaned back on the old couch, another bottle of wine already un-corked. The pool table from S's old basement lurked beneath its leather cover just behind the couch where my mother sat, and the large televi-sion I'd watched at his house as a child was pushed up against the wall. My mother clicked the remote with her free hand and a listings direc-tory loaded up on the screen. I had never been in that house before, so I hadn't expected any ghosts to appear. But then my mother said, "I remember you always liked this one." And when I glanced up from the greasy slice on my plate, I saw that she'd found *Halloween* playing on a late-night movie channel, the sight of Haddonfield sending me back to my father's house all those years ago.

The broadcast was already near the end of the film. Laurie Strode entering the dark and quiet house and calling out for her friends. Laurie climbing the stairs.

My mother was sitting with her ankles crossed on the cushion beside her, an old off-white robe pulled tight around her body. She let her head fall back against a blanket draped over the back of the couch, the plate of pizza crusts now pushed aside. She smiled in the direction of the TV, her eyes already a little cloudy from the wine. "It's so nice that you're here," she said again.

The memory stings now because of how infrequent my visits home had been. The tagline on a popular movie poster for the original *Halloween* is prominent against the otherwise entirely black background: "The Night *He* Came Home!"—referring to Michael's return to Haddonfield after many years away. He doesn't seem to have changed since his first appearance as a young boy with the dead eyes holding the bloody knife. He remains unabashedly himself despite all attempts by Dr. Loomis and others to rehabilitate him, and therein lies the horror of it all. But unlike Michael, who is compelled to return home to relive the horrors wrought by his childhood self, I avoid returning to my own Haddonfield. I make excuses about crowded airports and delayed planes during peak holiday travel seasons. I claim I'm strapped for cash. I've missed milestone birthdays and the weddings of old classmates, the funerals of my grandparents, the births of children who will never know my face. And I don't attend reunions. I've watched friends become acquaintances and then strangers. Something always keeps me from returning.

The twentieth anniversary of T's murder summoned her to mind after years of not thinking about her at all, her smiling face appearing suddenly while I scrolled through my social media feed in posts made by high school classmates whom I now barely recognize, the passage of time having made its mark. Everyone was sharing memories from back when T was still alive. Now she looks impossibly young, just an innocent child. A little girl posing with a baseball bat after a softball game, a big sister sitting cross-legged on a carpeted floor with her younger siblings, all of them smiling up at the camera. Then she is holding a cigarette while sitting on the hood of a car, probably only days or weeks before her murder, and she looks more like I'd remembered her in that picture—but only if I also remembered who I'd been at the time. How I'd wanted to be just like her. How I'd wanted to be chosen out of all the others just as she had been. Back then I thought I would die for just one moment like that.

"Do you remember the girl who was killed?" I asked my mother that night in her new house, the two of us sitting together in the dark. We hadn't spoken since Laurie discovered the bodies of her friends and unleashed her primal scream.

"I think she's the one who makes it," my mother said, gesturing at the screen where Laurie was running out into the yard, nursing her first wound from Michael's knife after a narrow escape. She calls for help at the locked front doors of neighbors' houses but realizes to her horror that no one is coming to her rescue. No one is going to help her. No one believes she's in any real danger—it's Halloween night, after all. Everyone is only pretending to be scared. None of it is supposed to be real.

Then Michael approaches from the dark front yard across the street, knife in hand.

"In my class," I clarified, still thinking of T as I watched Laurie. "When I was a kid."

"Of course," said my mother with a quick glance in my direction. She made an exaggerated shudder as she lit up another cigarette, pulling her robe tighter around her body against the chill in the air, a draft creeping in from the sliding door to the patio. "We were nearby the night the guy was found. The guy who killed her. The college near the old bowling alley where we used to take you guys on the weekends. Do you remember?"

"I remember," I said.

"Around the same time as your father," said my mother, surprising me by how easily she'd conjured up the memory. "Everything was about to change after that summer. I didn't know what to do with you anymore."

On the screen, Laurie was back in the house comforting the children after another brush with Michael, telling them that she had killed the bogeyman and that there's nothing to be afraid of anymore. But then he appears behind her at the top of the stairs.

My mother took a long drag of her cigarette, the smoke hovering above her head. "Sometimes I think I could've done something," she said. "Helped him out somehow. Maybe it would've made a difference. But I had you guys to look after, I was working all the time . . ."

She sighed and covered her mouth, coughing after another pull of the cigarette that had already burned down almost to the filter. She dropped it into the ashtray on the coffee table, the flame slowly dying out. My eyes were burning from the smoke, and I wasn't even looking at the screen when Michael attacks Laurie in the hallway and she fumbles helplessly with his mask, trying to reveal his face.

"What do you mean?" I asked. "What do you mean you could have helped him? He was so sick. What could you have done?"

"He used to tell me blonde jokes," my mother said, not really hearing me anymore. "Near the end. Years after the divorce. He would call me at work without even saying who he was, and he'd just tell me a blonde joke when I answered the phone. A different one each time. Three blondes walk into a bar," she said, chuckling to herself, and I tried to picture my mother at her desk at the accounting firm, fingers dancing across a calculator before she paused to pick up the phone and hear a joke from my father.

"I don't even know who found him," she said. "I don't think anyone ever told me. Maybe I didn't even ask."

Found. The word landed like a brick at my feet.

I could tell from her face that my mother wasn't fully with me in the room anymore. She had traveled back to that summer. "We were in Florida when it happened," she continued.

"The nurse, you mean?" I said, my voice strained. I could feel blood pulsing at my temples. "At the hospital? Why does it matter?"

My mother shook her head. "Maybe if someone had found him sooner, or if he'd just made it back to wherever he was staying—"

"I don't understand," I said sharply, interrupting her with my sudden confusion. My heart was racing and the smoke in the air seemed to have grown thicker, more dense and heavy, but my mother hadn't lit up another cigarette. Then I noticed that everything was spinning vaguely around me, as if we were on a carousel coming slowly to a halt. The old furniture lurking in the shadows was growing and then shrinking in size, the light playing tricks on me.

"He was driving home from a bar when it happened," said my mother.

I pictured my father behind the wheel of his car, glancing over at me in the passenger seat, a beer can nestled between his legs and all the empties crumpled at his feet. I remembered that sometimes on longer drives he would pull over to vomit out the open window after one too many beers, or maybe he would make it to a gas station trash can and then rinse his mouth with water from the restroom sink before he'd have me open another can for him from the case on the floor of the back seat as we resumed the drive. By then it was nighttime, and the headlights showed us what was coming just before we flew on past.

"He stopped on the side of the road," she continued, "and crawled out of the car. I don't know how far he made it. I don't know what he was looking for. He was probably already blacked out, already gone. But they didn't find him until a couple days later. You knew this," she continued, a question entering her voice for the first time. "I told you. I must have told you?"

My father died alone in a vacant lot somewhere near St. Louis where he'd been staying with friends after he lost the house where we'd all once lived together. He died after another night of drinking that ended as he looked up at the sky and waited for his heart to stop. We had been in Florida at the time, but now I was there with him in my mind as he counted down those final moments. I was there because I'd also been alone that summer on those long nights, waiting for whatever was coming for me. But I didn't know at the time that my father was there too. The headlights of other cars racing by late at night while he took his final breaths, no one stopping to see if he needed help. No one checking to see whether he could have been saved.

"You didn't tell me," I said to my mother then, rage blooming in my chest. No one had told me anything. The secret had been kept from me. And I was suddenly so angry that tears sprang to my eyes. I'd been made to spend all those years without knowing the truth about my father's death. How dare she leave me in the dark like that. All these things we don't tell each other.

I've imagined the scene many times before: we are seated on stools next to each other at a mostly empty bar, elbows on the counter and fingers curled around tall beer glasses sweating into white paper napkins. If my father were still alive, this is where I would find him. I can't imagine him being anywhere else. An empty pitcher is positioned between us on the counter, a muted ballgame playing on an elevated screen behind the row of bottles. My father and I absently lift our pints to our lips as classic rock from a nearby jukebox fills the silence that would otherwise hover between us, each waiting for the other to speak. My mother always said we had the same eyes, almost gray with quiet hints of blue. But my father never knew what mine had seen. He never knew the things I'd done.

In graduate school I wrote a piece for workshop about a boy wizard who discovers his magical powers only at the end of the story, when he looks back and realizes he'd once done something horrible without having known at the time. He remembers feeling angry at his father for not being there for him as a child, always out drinking somewhere, as if that was the only thing that mattered. One night the anger burns so brightly in him that his hands sear the wood beneath his palms as he presses hard against the windowsill in his bedroom and thinks about how he'd wanted a different father, a better father—how he would destroy his own father to turn him into something else. The boy wizard learns the next day that his father has died, that he'll never get a chance to make everything right. Now his anger doubles, triples, growing in size over the years that follow until it almost consumes him. Then as a teenager he realizes—when firebolts burst from his fingers as bullies chase him down a wooded street near his house, swiftly turning their bodies to ash—that he'd had these powers all along, and just hadn't known how to use them. He understands that he'd killed his father, too, on that long ago night with his uncontainable rage, the burning sensation in his hands only the aftereffect of the damage he'd already done. And the realization tears him apart, rewriting everything he'd ever known.

"You always had such a wild imagination," my mother continued as I refilled my glass, my hand trembling as I made a sloppy pour and red wine spilled down the stem onto the coffee table. "Do you remember how you were always so scared of the dark? You said it felt like someone was in there with you when I left you alone in your room. Someone in the shadows, someone you couldn't see. I remember thinking back then that you saw things none of us could. Like you were living in a whole different world."

Maybe the truth about my father would have been a warning sign along the highway on those nights when I drove into the city with the bottle of vodka beside me. Or maybe I would have thought of him in later years in other cities, the wild nights of bright lights and dance floors and shot after shot of house liquor from bartenders flashing quick smiles, the blur of late nights and after-hours parties ending only the morning after in a stranger's bed in a strange neighborhood. Most times I wouldn't remember his name the next morning or how we'd met, the events of the night before coming slowly back to me in hazy montage as I fumbled blindly for my clothes: stumbling through the dark and spitting bile into a toilet in the early morning hours when the buzz from the liquor had become a dull ache in the center of my forehead. Maybe the knowledge could have protected me somehow from all those men who had seen me where I'd been hiding in those years I spent in the dark. The years before I moved away from home. Men like the one at the pool in Florida who noticed me for what I was and didn't pretend they hadn't, no matter how young I was. A boy afraid of something in himself and men who knew he would do anything they asked, if only they wouldn't tell. If only they would keep the secret of him.

"This part always stayed with me after I first watched it," said my mother as she looked anxiously over at the TV screen, her voice pulling me back to her. Somehow I'd already emptied my wine glass. "I was just a teenager. I watched it with your father when we first started dating. I was just sixteen when it came out. And I would get these nightmares . . ." Her voice trailed off as she shook her head from side to side as if to ward off those old demons.

Laurie is cowering on the hallway floor. I hadn't been watching when the gunshots were fired and Michael stumbled through the open window. Now Dr. Loomis has looked out the window and discovered that Michael somehow survived the bullet wounds and the fall and has disappeared once again into the night. Laurie begins to sob, burying her face in her bloody hands. She would forever be looking over her shoulder for the bogeyman. She would never be safe again. He would always be coming for her.

My mother was studying my face in the dim light. "I can't believe you didn't know what happened," she said, and I knew she was thinking about my father again. She frowned and took another gulp of wine. "You were always watching. Always listening."

I'd been right when I assumed my father had been drunk when we spoke on the phone for the last time before we left for Florida, slurring his words even in the morning hours as he asked me how things were going at camp, saying my name too loudly when I took the receiver from my mother, her lips pressed tightly together. I hadn't wrongfully condemned him, hadn't misread the clues. The cancer had never returned after all. But I also hadn't really understood the bogeyman. The bogeyman had already been with us on the drives my brother and I took with our father late at night when the car swerved dangerously and I'd instinctively grab the door handle until the direction had been corrected. The bogeyman was with my father when I watched *Halloween* for the first time in his living room while he sat at the kitchen table as the beer cans accumulated. The bogeyman had been outside with him when I perused the aisles at the video store, eventually landing upon Michael Myers.

The bogeyman had been watching us the whole time.

The mandate of a character in a horror film is not revelation or epiphany but simply the fact of a body moving through space and stumbling blindly through the dark. Rarely does the ending offer any kind of consolation. There are always loose ends, something not quite right. A monster sinking to the bottom of the lake. The distant clanging of chains in the attic. A bogeyman vanishing into the night. That night with my mother, I made myself watch as *Halloween* was about to end, and as the camera cut away from its final glimpses of Laurie and Dr. Loomis, I was struck for the first time by the final moments of the film—images I'd overlooked until then.

Following the revelation that Michael has escaped into the night and that the citizens of Haddonfield are still in danger, the camera lingers on the interior domestic spaces that now seem sinister and dangerous because of Michael's former intrusions. As if he's perhaps still there, lying in wait behind the couch or the living room curtains or appearing suddenly at the top of a dark staircase. The last things we see are static images of the Haddonfield houses in which the acts of violence have been committed. First, there's the Doyle house, its multiwindowed façade partially obscured by the lightly rustling leaves on tree branches casting long shadows over the yard, where Laurie had gone to babysit Tommy and where she later had her final confrontation with Michael. Then there's the Wallace house across the street with only the porch light still on, the windows all dark. The smiling jack-o'-lantern on the front porch is the only evidence that anyone lives there, the flame of the candle behind its mouth flickering in the faint autumn breeze.

Finally, there's the old Myers house. The dark upstairs windows loom large above the empty front porch like a pair of eyes peering menacingly out onto the streets and sidewalks of Haddonfield—the house like the face of the devil, exactly how Loomis had once described Michael himself. All the lights are off inside each of these houses, and we can't see in through any of the darkened windows, but we now know what might be lurking just beyond those seemingly inviting front doors. We know that what seems innocuous and benign on the outside can in fact contain deadly secrets, horrors that have been locked away. We aren't innocent anymore.

While I watched those houses flash before me in the dark as the ending credits rolled, my mother groped for the remote control to lower the volume as the soundtrack began to play and the three houses of my own childhood appeared unbidden in my mind as if I'd never left them behind. The house where I woke up during the storm and then later to protect my mother from my father. The townhouse we moved into after the divorce, where I'd spent so many sleepless nights and where I saw the man in the hallway who'd paused in the dim light before walking to the bathroom, giving shape to what before then had been only the outline of a desire—a pencil drawing waiting for color. And then the house where I'd been unable to sleep on those long nights after my father's death, just lying awake and staring at the ceiling and waiting for whatever was going to come for me next.

I remembered that in those dark hours I would picture what the house looked like from the outside. At first glance it was just another modest two-story on a tiny plot of land in a row of others just like it, a quiet neighborhood where young children often played in the street until dusk. But mine was the only upstairs bedroom window that faced the road, and I wondered whether anyone could tell from the outside that someone like me was living there. Whether the house had somehow been marked by what I'd brought inside with me. And in the early morning hours, long before dawn but after the rest of the house had fallen soundly asleep around me, the memory of the man in Florida would resurface just as I finally allowed myself the pleasure of my own touch. No matter how hard I tried to banish him from my mind, there he was again, keeping me company in the dark, the sight of his body exposed above me in the water clearly free for the taking while I hesitated there beneath the surface, not yet knowing in those first shocked moments what I would do in response.

"You were so angry that summer," my mother was saying. She reached for the bottle of wine and then noticed with a sigh that it was already empty. "You wouldn't leave your room. Sometimes I'd knock and knock and say your name over and over again and you wouldn't even answer. You wouldn't ever come to the door."

She clicked off the TV with the remote control, and then we could see only our own faces reflected back to us on the empty screen. My mother and myself. The image was distorted and vague, the shapes of our bodies stretched either too thin or too wide, the portrait almost conceptual in its exaggeration of certain details. Everything else mostly in shadow.

"You were so mad at the world after your dad was gone," she continued. "But you wouldn't talk about it. I thought maybe I'd been wrong to keep you from him at the end. Maybe we didn't try hard enough to make it work." She sighed again. "And then he was just gone."

She finished the last of her wine, tipping up the glass by the stem.

"I thought you blamed me for what happened to your father," she said. "But I didn't know how to talk to you about it. You would scream if I tried to come in your room. You would punch the wall until I thought it would cave in. Sometimes I worried you'd take the whole house down with you."

But I hadn't been thinking only about my father that summer in the days and weeks following his funeral. The violence bubbling up inside me came from somewhere else. My father's death had not been what haunted me most. Only later could I travel back in my mind and make space for him in that room where I'd locked myself away.

That night with my mother, I finally understood that he had also been walking down his own long hallway toward whatever was waiting for him at the end, but he'd made it there before I did. The man waiting for me in the dream had always been so far away in the distance, just a vague shape in the dark. But his face was a mask I'd fill in with the evidence of all the long years I'd have to put behind me until I eventually became him—a man who had made it to the other side and somehow survived the treacherous journey after all the damage had been done. As the darkness deepened around me, every miserable step that I took alone was more difficult and more dangerous than the last, the lost and frightened boy walking further and further into the unknown even as something deep inside screamed for him to turn around and run back to where he came from, to look away and never again be tempted by whatever was waiting for him.

All the way back to when he was just a little boy in a video store who knew nothing about Michael Myers or Haddonfield. A little boy who had not yet glimpsed the bogeyman.

I knew after the trip to Florida that I wouldn't be able to keep my secret forever. After all, the man at the pool had known right away. He hadn't needed to take a second look to know what I was. The mark I bore could not be scrubbed clean but instead would fester like a wound. The fact of it made me seethe with a fury I've never known since. I hadn't asked for any of this. And even though I disgusted myself and wanted to wipe clean the mess my dirty thoughts had made, I still fantasized relentlessly that summer about what might have happened if I hadn't run away that day at the resort. What might have happened if I'd done everything I imagined that the man at the pool might have offered me.

I follow him to an empty room just off the courtyard, photographs of seashells in cheap frames on the yellow wall, a painting of a horizon at sunset hung at a slight tilt above the unmade bed. He turns off the lights, draws the thick curtains, and steps toward me in the dark. I'm already hard when he grabs me by the shoulders and throws me over to the bed before scrambling toward me across the sagging mattress, his body now heavy on top of mine as he tugs my wet swim shorts down to my ankles. I can feel how much he wants me by the way he takes me without asking. I can feel how much he wants me by the way he is not gentle at all. In the fantasy, I'm not twelve years old anymore. I'm not trying to get away. He isn't doing anything wrong. After all, I'd been begging for it. Everyone had seen.

My mother stood up and her feet found the slippers waiting beside her on the floor as she tied the belt of her robe, tucking the mostly empty pack of cigarettes into her pocket. She told me that she would have given anything to know what I'd been thinking about back then. She wished she could have helped.

"You were right there," she said, "but you felt so far away."

Then she was saying something else about that summer, something that she had just remembered about me. But a violent wave of dizziness flooded my head, everything spinning in the darkness past the couch and the now empty TV screen. The unfamiliar shadows of a house I did not know. I couldn't hear anything my mother was saying anymore. The wine churned in my stomach as it rushed up to my chest and burned the base of my throat as I stumbled blindly from the couch through the darkness toward the basement bathroom I'd been shown earlier. I couldn't find the light switch and I lurched toward the toilet in the dark, my knees buckling beneath me as I heaved and spat and tried to still my trembling hands, my mouth still foul with bile and the sour taste of the wine.

I don't know how long I spent in the bathroom, but I finally managed to grip the edge of the countertop and pull myself up to take several long gulps of water that I cupped directly into my hands from the faucet, my knees searing with pain from when I had collapsed onto the tiled floor. I splashed my face and stared for a long moment at my ghostly reflection in the dark, hoping that meeting my own gaze would anchor me as I waited for the world to steady itself around me. But the face in the glass was a stranger again, someone I didn't know.

When I stepped shakily back out into the basement shadows, I saw the outline of my mother ahead of me in the dark, waiting at the bottom of the stairs where the single bulb of an overhead light would guide her up into her new house. I knew she'd heard everything.

"Are you okay now?" she asked. But I could only stand there slumped against the doorframe, not trusting what I might have said in response.

Soon I would follow her up into the house I didn't know and find my way to a spare bed. My brother's old bed, the top bunk I'd slept in at the townhouse having been removed long ago so that only the single twin bedframe remained—the same bed where he'd cowered from me that summer day when my rage had threatened to bring the house down around us. And when I finally made it upstairs, I would also notice my old dresser shoved into the corner of the guest bedroom, the desk against the wall with my initials notched into the cheap wood of the top drawer where I'd sat and written my first short stories as a child. Monsters of my own invention, little boys who only sometimes managed to escape.

And there I was again, as if I'd never left at all.

But I wanted to linger awhile in the dark, and I didn't move from the bathroom doorway as my mother turned the corner and finally disappeared from view. At some point I heard the door at the top of the stairs click shut, her footsteps retreating across the hardwood floor of the living room after she'd rinsed our wine glasses at the kitchen sink. Water in the pipes as she brushed her teeth and washed her face, the hard yank of the pull chain on her bedside lamp. And then the house was finally quiet. I listened to the silence for a while, wondering when I'd hear S's car pulling into the garage and the kitchen door slamming shut as he came inside. Or maybe he'd already come home, while my mother and I were talking, and we just hadn't noticed. After all, the conversation had been like a kind of time travel, and I hadn't yet made my way fully back to the present. I was still somewhere in between.

In the deepening quiet I remembered the train whistle that I used to wait for late at night at the old house, the comfort I'd felt after hearing proof that someone else was awake out there just like me. How I'd listen for hours just to hear that long note sounding out over all the quiet houses with their shades pulled tight, a sad and lonely call in the thick darkness making me want to run out of the house and follow close behind on its journey to wherever it was going. Even though it would be years before I finally could.

A shape appeared suddenly in the near darkness, approaching me from beside the couch where I'd been sitting with my mother, a prowling menace creeping out of the shadows. My body went taut as I registered the potential threat. I thought again about Michael Myers—how he was always still out there, always watching and waiting. And I knew for sure that something had finally come for me after all those years, something evil that had just been waiting and gathering its power for when I'd finally return and make myself vulnerable once again to its steady advance. Maybe I'd always known it would happen, and that was why I'd stayed away all that time. The horrors I'd seen in Haddonfield would finally be made real and I would succumb in that dark basement just like all the others, the people in my dream and the girls being chased through the streets on a night they never could have imagined would end this way. Girls like T.

Now I didn't know where to hide. I didn't have the strength to defend myself. I wouldn't have been able to make myself run.

But then I saw that what had frightened me there in the dark was just one of my mother's cats, probably having woken up from a nap to inspect the stranger lurking in its home. After all, I was the one who didn't belong. I was the one who had brought danger into the house, the unfamiliar shape that had made the small creature afraid. I caught its eye for a moment, a brief flash of gold as it sized me up, and I released a breath I didn't even know I'd been holding when it finally looked away. Then the cat must have retreated to wherever it had come from, because there was no more movement in the deepening shadows. I was alone again, my trembling hands groping along the wall toward the staircase.

One step forward and then another. Morning was still hours away.

Acknowledgments

I'm grateful to so many people, first and foremost my family, who share these pages with me. Many thanks to Matthew Cheney for invaluable feedback and encouragement. To my writing groups for reading early drafts: Sarra Alpert, Katherine Carlson, Doug Dibbern, Tania Friedel, Austin Kelley, Beth Machlan, Amira Pierce, Jenni Quilter, and Leeore Schnairsohn. And to my teachers: Nathan Englander, Helen Schulman, Darin Strauss, and Colson Whitehead. To Melissa Amstutz, Amy Cassell, and Sara Webster—we'll always have Paris. Thanks also to Lee Cohen, Alex Guillen, Paul Lisicky, and Cassie Mannes Murray. To Danielle Halley and Keith Sabalja, for our scary movie nights and so much more. And to John Carpenter and Debra Hill for *Halloween*.

I'm grateful for fellowships from MacDowell and the New York Foundation for the Arts. Thanks also to the Virginia Center for the Creative Arts, Vermont Studio Center, and La Porte Peinte for the time and space to work on this book. Thanks to *Electric Literature*, where words from these pages first appeared, and to Joe Vallese and the team at the Feminist Press for anthologizing that earlier piece. And I owe so much gratitude to my colleagues at the Expository Writing Program at New York University for their invaluable support over the years.

Finally, many thanks to the amazing team at the University of Wisconsin Press who helped usher this book into the world with such consideration and care. To Zelda, who waited for me to finish. And to Ed Gonzalez, for everything.

LIVING OUT

Gay and Lesbian Autobiographies

DAVID BERGMAN, JOAN LARKIN, and RAPHAEL KADUSHIN,
Founding Editors

The Change: My Great American, Postindustrial, Midlife Crisis Tour
LORI SODERLIND

Outbound: Finding a Man, Sailing an Ocean
WILLIAM STORANDT

Given Up for You: A Memoir of Love, Belonging, and Belief
ERIN O. WHITE